HELL'S DAUGHTER

TRINITY-ROSE
CRANE

JP

This paperback edition published 2020 by Jasami Publishing Ltd
an imprint of Jasami Publishing Ltd
Glasgow, Scotland
https://jasamipublishingltd.com

ISBN 978-1-913798-10-9

Copyright © Trinity-Rose Crane 2020
Illustration & Artwork Copyright © Holly Richards 2020

All rights reserved. No part of this publication may be reproduced, stored in a retrieval system, or transmitted, in any form, or by any means (electronic, mechanical, photocopying, recording or otherwise) without the prior written permission of the publisher except for brief quotations used for promotion or in reviews.

All stories are original, all names, characters, and incidents portrayed in this are fictitious. No identification with actual persons (living or deceased), places, buildings, and products is intended or should be inferred.

Visit JasamiPublishingLtd.com to read more about all our books and to purchase them. You will also find features, author information and news of any events, also be the first to hear about our new releases.

ACKNOWLEDGEMENTS

First I would like to thank Michele Smith because without her having faith in my work this book wouldn't exist and for guiding me through the writer to author experience.

May for all her work on editing it to make it perfect.

Holly Richards for introducing me to Jasami Publishing and for the amazing art work and bringing the book to life. All the illustrations are better than I could ask for. I especially love all the special extra details.

My older sisters for letting me talk out plot points with them and my little sister for wanting to read my book but not being old enough.

My grandparents for being very enthusiastic about my book and promoting it to everyone they meet.

My best friend Jessica for being amazing and dealing with me for thirteen years and counting.

To the owners at Bubble Drop for not judging how many times I went to get bubble tea from their van to help me write.

And lastly, my dog for regularly barking at me to take breaks and play ball with her.

DEDICATION

To my parents who would answer any questions I had about stabbing techniques, knives and wounds without asking any follow up questions likewise I never asked how they always knew the answers.

CHAPTER ONE

Abby

The lesson ends, I have no more lessons today. I am free! Swinging on my backpack, I sigh in relief. I don't think I could take another lesson. A hand grabs my arm, I pray it's not a teacher trying to keep me behind, I turn.

"Abby." Thankfully, my friend, Kyle, stands before my eyes.

"Hi." I grin.

Kyle is the typical good-looking guy around here. He has hair down to his shoulders which he can barely pull off. I keep trying to convince him to get it cut, it'll look better I swear. His eyes are trusting, a soft hazel colour with flecks of soft brown. There have been suspicions we have dated, but we never have and never will. We've been best friends for years.

"Are you going to the party tomorrow?" His eyes dance mischievously.

"Or course." We walk out of the classroom, unbothered by the teachers, to the rich taste of freedom. I never miss a party, no matter who throws it. This time it's a boy in our year called Colt. I don't really know who he is but it's a party for everyone in twelfth grade.

Hell's Daughter

We walk out the rusty high school gates, where we meet Kyle's girlfriend, Lily. Instantly, she pecks his cheek and their hands intertwine. I make loud wrenching sounds beside them. I laugh under their dual glower in my direction. It's sweet, really. I chuckle, the sun bathes my face. I swear the windows in school reflect light. Or the school just sucks away the light like it sucks away our will to live. Kyle's eyes light up simply at the sight of Lily. I don't blame him, she is even hotter than he is. The three of us walk down the silent street, the rest of the students have dispersed. We are going to hang out at the park, my sister is meeting us there. We are non-identical twins. We look nothing alike. It's almost comical. No-one ever suspects it. They think our matching last names are a coincidence. I have dark hair, a sharp jawline, piercing green eyes and average height. My sister is blonde, hazel eyes, tall with soft facial features. She looks like the definition of an angel, and I the devil. Or that's what my parents joke. I open my mouth, looking around I realise, I am walking alone.

I spin, calling out their names. I know exactly what they are doing. They are making out against the wall completely forgetting my existence. I sigh. "Hello?" I wave.

I don't mind the concept of relationships but at least don't ignore me completely. I get no response. I roll my eyes, I was hoping we could make it to the park before this happened. I turn around and carry on, alone. No doubt my sister will be late. She'll be too busy snogging her girlfriend. I respect that they have relationships, but I find parties a lot more fun when you aren't attached to another person. I waltz over to the park, no point racing there when I'll be first to arrive.

Collapsing onto the grass, under the shade of a tree, I can still smell old dew on the grass from past rainfalls. I stretch out, the ache in my bones from being cramped under a desk, slowly releasing. My hair falls over my face and I bat it away carelessly. My jeans hug my legs and my cropped shirt reveals a few inches of my stomach. I wear white sneakers, not the best idea I'll admit as they are already stained with mud.

"Abby, where are Kyle and Lily?" My sister asks, approaching.

"Where do you think?" I pat the space next to me for her to sit.

Our styles are completely different, she wears loose jeans, with frayed ends and a baggy, blue sweater. Her hands disappear in the sleeves. "Where's Selena?"

"Busy." Holly sighs sadly, fingers playing with the loose threads of her sleeves.

"Are you both coming to the party?" I shade my eyes from the sun.

"Yes." She begins pulling out grass strands instead of her worn sweater.

My eyes widen, I thought I would have to convince her. "Really?"

"Selena wants to go."

Well, that explains it, it is normally Selena who can persuade her. I'm rather useless at it.

"Okay, remember it's a pool party so wear a bikini under the sweater."

A sigh. "Oh, Abby!"

"What? Fine. You don't have to wear one but I am. They'll be hot boys there. I need to look good." I argue.

"I don't understand single people." My sister chuckles. "So damn desperate all the time."

"Hey! I'm not desperate!" I shove her playfully.

Half an hour later, no one arrives. They forgot about us, it wouldn't have been the first time. We stand up and leave the park. All our homework is done, Holly insisted. It's not how I'd want to spend my time. The chance that I actually do my homework is only fifty percent. I have better things to do with my time. Holly gets much better grades than I do, she's all the

Hell's Daughter

teachers' favourite, not a teacher's pet but they like her much more than they like me. I can't blame them, to be honest. I am not the best-behaved student.

The next day, I flip through my clothes pulling out an outfit. I'm wearing a bikini already. It's olive green and simple. I pick out the clothes. My usual ripped jeans but tighter than normal and a shirt. The shirt drops at the front and reaches halfway down my stomach and is the same colour as my bikini, so it doesn't clash. Lucky for us, our parents are away on a trip for their twentieth wedding anniversary which means we have no curfew for the party. A knock on my bedroom door, and opening it. I see my sister's outfit.

"You are not wearing that." I point to it.

"Why not?"

"Look at it!" I shake my head disapprovingly.

Holly wears a dress, it goes past her knees and has less shape than a sack of potatoes. In her hand, a sweater with holes in it. That makes it three times worse, especially because it is a different colour to the dress. She has her hair in a messy bun which at least looks nice.

"Come here." I grab her wrist.

"We have to go!" Holly resists.

"We have ten minutes. Please. Selena will love it." I pull her in my room and start pulling out clothes for her to try on.

Ten minutes later, Holly is ready; she has resisted make-up but wears the dress I chose for her. Not tight but shows her off, and a matching denim jacket. I pull on my favourite leather jacket, and buckle on high heels.

"Let's go," I announce.

"If we are late, I'm blaming you." She grumbles, even though she is stroking the denim jacket's sleeve. She likes the outfit but just won't admit it.

I roll my eyes, looking once more in the mirror. I pull a strand of curly hair out of my bun. "There!" I don't know why I put the effort in my hair, it's a pool party. It'll get wet and be ruined. At least I will look good when I walk in.

Reaching the party, it is already raving. Lights, music and bodies. All packed and dancing up against one another. A cheer in the distance from a group playing beer pong. People are already in the pool. A mixture of sweat, chlorine, and alcohol weaves through the air. It is hardly a pleasant smell. Kyle is holding on to Lily by her waist. Holly and Selena hold hands. Selena complimented Holly's outfit the second she saw her in it. I knew she would.

"Come on. It's a party. Mingle." I urge them.

"How about we go to the wood over there." Selena offers to Holly, and points to the forest behind the house, away from the party.

"Are you serious?" I spin, but they are gone. "What about you two?" I ask.

"I'm always up for a party. Dance with me?" Lily pulls Kyle away.

"Don't ditch me!" I call, but they are gone.

I sigh, helping myself to a beer. The house is nice, very large. The pool was made for pool parties. Lights are strung above it. I venture into the party alone. The home is at the edge of town, a forest surrounding the garden. Colt's parents are very wealthy and are very relaxed if they are letting this happen. If he is doing this without their knowledge, I feel bad for all the mess he is going to have to clean up after, so he doesn't leave any trace.

After my second beer, I dance along with the crowd. My hair flies wildly out my bun, I haven't talked to many people, I will probably join a game of beer pong later once I find some people I know. Currently, I dance with a boy, his blonde hair falling in his face, smiling tipsily. His grey eyes are beautiful and glazy. I grin back, we sway back and forth. Music drums through my ears, loud enough to burst my eardrums. I can't hear the words he tries to say, I lean closer and yell. "What?" Praying he would hear.

He frowns, wrapping his fingers around my forearm and pulls me away from the crowd. The music grows faint as we get further away. We reach the edge of the party, a few people leaning on trees talking. We are near the house. There are very few people inside the building.

"I said, are you single?" He mutters, lips next to my ear.

"Hell yes."

Is that even a question? It's very easy to tell who is dating at a party. They cling to one another and don't let go.

That answer is all he needed. Our lips connect desperately and I grab the back of his head. Drawing him in. He tastes of vodka, smoke and mint. My gut explodes in fireworks. His hands touch my back, icy against my skin. I shiver. My lips burn against his cold ones. I taste blood, irony and sweet. He kisses me harder, till he draws back for a breath. I gasp for air.

"I bit you!" He panics, it was my lip that is bleeding.

"Oh." I touch my lip gently, that explains the blood taste.

"Are you okay?" He touches my lip gently in concern.

I smile, pulling him back by his jacket. "Yes."

A sideways grin, his teeth shining in the moonlight. "Good." He relaxes.

We kiss again as furiously as before. Drawing back, he whispers in my ear. "You are an amazing kisser."

"I know," I admit.

He rolls his eyes. "What's your name?"

"Abby."

"Colt."

"Well, Colt, you're not too bad either." I flirt shamelessly.

"I know." He grins, going in for more.

A scream erupts over the blaring music. We jump apart, glancing at one another. The sound came from the forest. Even the deafening music could not overpower the agonising screams. Who?

"Help! Please!" Selena rushes into the party, holding someone drenched in blood. I know who that is. My breathing hitches. Holly. A wolf snaps, charging in after them.

Holy shit. Where in the devil did the wolf come from?

Rushing forward, I grab for Selena. I barely have time to process as the wolf pounces at me. I dodge, just making it to them. In Selena's arms my sister is unconscious, pale and soaked in blood. Forcing Selena to lower her to the ground, I yank off my jacket to wrap it around the wound. Gasping, my sister howls out in pain. I tighten the makeshift bandage.

"Call an ambulance!" I scream. Holly stirs in my arms. A soft groan. "Holly please wake up!" I beg. I can't feel my phone in my pocket. Selena is already dialling.

"No!" A voice calls.

The wolf leaps in our direction. Colt jumps in the way. The wolf snaps at him. Swiftly, I grab a log of firewood from the bonfire and hold it like a bat. Thoughtlessly, I swing. A crack, the bat connects with its head. A yelp, it rolls off Colt. Tears burn on my face, my hands are shaking. The wolf jumps again, razor-sharp teeth snapping. I swing, I knock it hard. Sending it skittering for the water's edge.

"Stay back!" I howl, panic and adrenaline pumping in my veins. I point the log dangerously, splinters falling off. Slipping, the paws tap on the side of the pool. Everyone has evacuated the pool and the party. The noise is deafening. Groups running away as fast as they can. Yellow eyes bore into my own, the thick brown fur coat damp. I'm frozen.

Suddenly, its teeth wrap around the log, it tugs. What do I do? In my moment of hesitation, we both tumble into the pool. Water enveloping overhead. The cold rush, throbs in my body. The wolf is a soggy, furry mess. Its claws are rising. I scream for help. Bubbles of oxygen leaving my mouth. That was a bad idea. The wolf grabs my ankle. I shriek, we sink. Fighting for freedom

Hell's Daughter

in blind desperation. Chlorine burning my eyes. I wail. The surface seems so close, just out of reach. I cry out, frantically swimming upward. My lungs burn. I let out my breath too soon. I need oxygen. A blur, blonde hair gets between me and the wolf. My head hits the surface... I gasp. Water pouring out my mouth. I wheeze.

"Are you okay?"

Blinking hard, my vision blurs. Barely able to see the face ahead. I am unable to speak. I cough up pools of water. Looking up, I see dark hair, dripping wet. I smile weakly, my throat burning. I am panting for breath but I can't seem to find it.

"Hi…" My eyes droop shut.

Gasping, I wake up from my nightmare. I shiver. I'm not in my bedroom. I'm at the poolside. It was real. I wheeze. I passed out.

"Holly!" I whimper voice hoarse.

"It's okay. She's on her way to the hospital." Colt appears, passing over a mug.

I hold the steaming mug in my ice-cold hands. The stench of chlorine and blood clings to my body and clothes. "I need to see her."

"She's fine." Colt insisted, looking deep in my eyes. "Believe me."

My heart thuds in my chest, and I believe him. I don't know why, but I do.

"We need you to stay here."

I nod, my sister is okay. I sit back in my seat. My shoulders relax, yet I still feel tense. A man, possibly in his early twenties glares down at me, arms folded angrily.

"Who are you?" I ask.

Enzo

I knew I shouldn't have let Colt throw the party. Staring down at the girl, my brows furrow. I don't like her. Shivering, she holds onto the mug for dear life. Colt sits in front of her, talking gently. The girl's sodden hair drips down her bare shoulders. The jeans she wears cling to her, even more, if that's possible. One of my hoodies keeps her warm. Colt steps back from her shaking human body. Looking up, she realises that I'm standing here. "Who are you?" She asks.

"Enzo." My eyes narrow.

She nods slowly as if she needs time to process the name.

Grabbing Colt's arm, I lean in to whisper to him. "Don't tell her anything. She didn't see enough. We can lie." I growl.

Colt yanks back, angrily. "Her sister got bitten! It's only a matter of time."

"I'm not dumb. We tell the sister, not this human."

"She deserves to know what will happen to her sister."

I scowl. Colt never understands, he lets his emotions in too often. They take control.

"She is human." I hiss the reminder. "You know what happens to humans."

"Not this time." Colt argues. "She has us."

"Us?" I ask, wondering if I heard right. I am not included in this.

"Fine, me. She'll have me." Colt eyes flare in defiance.

"What is going on?" Abby snaps.

I can't stop Colt, he is reckless and new. He must learn his lessons the hard way. And I will be there to pick up the mess that he makes of it. "Are you sure?"

"Yes."

I growl, tensing. I can tell Abby is an irresponsible child. And human no less. She could die, or worse. Yes, she might have beaten down a wolf but she wouldn't have lived through that if Colt hadn't intervened. She would be dead, and we would be discussing where to put her body right now. My hair is still wet from dragging her out of the pool. My jaw holds a bruise where she punched back in retaliation. It was tempting to let her drown, very tempting. But, Colt would have been mad. I consider it. Taking a deep breath. "She'll have us."

Colt smiles, happy to win the battle. "Good."

"Don't smile. I hate the idea, but I won't let you die."

"Modest much? Don't think I could live without you, huh?"

"No. You would be dead if it wasn't for me, long dead."

"I could say the same." He grins.

He's wrong, he's the modest one. I'd still be on this earth, with or without him. Turning, he looks back at Abby.

Colt bends down in front of her, getting in eye level. "Abby?"

"Yes?" She looks calm, thanks to Colt. He has a way with people, I do not.

"What I'm about to tell you, you cannot repeat to anyone else."

Abby is frowning. "Okay?"

"Promise," I growl. The promise doesn't mean anything. If she tells, she tells. I can't do much about it. I mean I could get her to promise on something or someone. I could make their demise happen if she broke her promise. Colt would think that is too extreme.

"I promise." Abby rolls her eyes.

"The wolf that attacked you and your sister..." Colt hesitates for a moment, as if he is considering what he is to say. "It was a werewolf."

I count to three in my head, then the laughter starts. Full-on belly laughter, that has her rolling and tea spilling all over the concrete. I'm glad we aren't inside; my poor white couch would be suffering otherwise. Hair bobbing, rocking back and forth. I roll my eyes. She hasn't sobered up yet I see. Scooping up a forgotten cup of water I dump the contents over her. She gasps, in shock. That should do it. If not, I will get more water.

"Enzo!" Colt snaps. "Don't throw water on her!"

"She was wet anyway." I shrug, the only fault in my plan is that my hoodie is wet now. I should have thought of that.

"You are serious?" Abby takes a moment to breathe shuddering from the cold. At least I got results.

"Yes." Colt nods. "And your sister got bitten which means..."

"You think she's a werewolf?! Did you hit your head?"

"No."

"Hmm—" Abby considers the possibility. Instantly ranking it at zero. I suspected so. "I think I'll leave now."

"No!" Colt grabs her arm in panic. He will need something big to make her stay and believe we are not a pair of crazy druggies. She wrenches her arm away. In desperation he splutters. "I'm a vampire."

She pauses. That can't be the convincing argument that gets her to stop. Colt really should think before he acts. "Is that why you bit me?"

Colt bit her? Of course, he did. That explains why he's so smitten after knowing her for only an hour. He's got human blood in his veins. He'll be a happy vampire for the next few hours before realising what a stupid idea this is. Human blood is like a drug for vampires. Pig blood is the best for vampires. It contains all the nutrients they need.

Abby's eyes meet mine. "What are you?"

"What I am, is none of your business." I quip.

"Enzo!" Colt hisses.

"All you need to know is I could kill you in a second with a snap of my fingers," I answer honestly.

"He is a hybrid. Part Warlock, part Hellhound." Colt also answers truthfully. "Though sometimes I think he's part goblin."

"And all the time I think you are all stupid." I retort.

"So, you believe. That the supernatural exists." She waves around vaguely. "And my sister is now a werewolf. I really don't know if you are insane, high, or serious."

"Colt! Fangs!" I order, trying to pick up the mess Colt is making. No-one will believe without proof.

Hell's Daughter

"I don't want to scare her."

He should have thought of that before deciding to tell her. If we can't convince her, she'll tell everyone about the mad people at the party who told her it was a werewolf that bit her sister. Then one curious human will seek answers and possibly get the answer. We can't have that happen. Humans don't cope well with it, the fact Colt is telling her is absurd. He doesn't truly understand, hopefully, this will be a good lesson. Sadly, we have to finish what Colt started.

Abby stares at us in confusion. I grab the back of her head. In her mind, I replay a scene. One of my memories. We jolt into an alleyway. A howl, a fiery hound, me, battling a demon. The dark goo oozing from its skin. The hideous creature with shark-like teeth. This is a favourite of mine. I always love to watch it over again. Feel my teeth tear the leathery skin. The horrific mushy tar taste of demon blood catches on my tongue. My claws, scarring the skin. Sending the demi-demon into a frenzy of pain. It burns into a pile of ash before my eyes. The dark ash scattering on the ground, blowing away in the wind. I grin in satisfaction. I remove my fingers from her head. I release her from my memory and get out of her mind. I watch her reaction, I got through to her.

Abby

Shivering, I hold myself in the enormous comfy hoodie. Enzo looms, sparks sizzling on his fingertips. The images flickering in my mind. My stomach churning, I want to throw up. I can still picture the tar substance oozing and bubbling through the crumbling skull. Wolfish jaws chomping down on the monster. The broken human-like body collapsing in the fiery jaws. Enzo kills it, biting in the rotting flesh. I can smell the smoke, the meat cooking to a crisp. I throw up, the vomit splashing into the pool. I wheeze, another load of vomit. All the food I ate today churning in my stomach and coming up. I taste vomit. My head spins more, what the hell did I just see? The wolf was on fire. I keep seeing it replaying in my head. My eyes go wide in disbelief, my sister is a werewolf.

"Do you believe us?" Enzo asks.

"Y-y-y-yes." I try to form words. "Wha-was—" It's true. All true. That image was enough. How did he do that? I could no longer see the pool or the concrete, it felt like I was there. It was horrifying.

"A demon."

"You're lucky the werewolf didn't get you." Colt waves to the scratch marks in my torn jeans.

"Did you tell Holly?" My eyes go wide in panic.

"No, not yet. They had her in the ambulance before we could reach her."

A nod. "Will I have to tell her?"

"If you want. Otherwise, we can." Colt offers, his cold hand touching mine.

I draw back. The freezing skin sending shivers down my spine. Colt drops my hand.

Taking a deep breath. "I'll tell Holly. How do I get her to believe me?"

"I'll come with you." Colt insists. "I can prove it."

I nod, sipping what is left of the drink, trying to drown out the taste of vomit. My teeth clink on the china cup. "Can we go inside?"

Enzo stares off into the distance through the window, tilting his head. Ignoring us. He lies back in a large armchair. He doesn't seem to want me here.

"Do you have any questions?" Colt watches the cup judder, sadness in his eyes. Can they sense fear?

"Too many. I—Is there a manual or something?" I take a deep breath, it's scary but also exciting. To know the supernatural exists. But what is it really? I love vampire movies, I love haunted movies. What parts of it are true? Colt isn't draining my body of blood. Enzo isn't doing whatever he can do. What is the truth? Enzo snaps his fingers; a worn brown leather book appears in his hand. The spine is tattered and old. I resist the urge to flinch at its touch. It looks older than my grandparents. I wonder if it feels like the demon's skin. It looks very similar. The pages seem slightly torn from usage. "Thank you."

Enzo grunts. I tuck the book on my lap. "I want to see Holly."

"We'll go soon," Colt promises, sipping his own mug.

Definitely not tea, it has red around the rim. "Is that blood?"

"Pig's blood, not human."

I could not tell the difference honestly. I decided to trust him on that one. I have no reason not to. He's told me the truth so far. "Why are you helping us?"

"Because we want to." Colt answers.

Enzo grunts in disagreement in the background. I assume he's only here for Colt.

"Why should I trust you?" I feel I should ask.

Enzo raises his eyebrow. "I saved your life. I could have let that werewolf eat you like it tried to do to your sister."

My lips tremble, remembering Holly. Blood soaking her, unconscious and vulnerable. "Sorry, thank you."

Enzo shrugs.

Colt glares his way. "We want to help you." Colt digs in his pocket and produces a phone. "I'll give you my number in case you need me."

"Thanks." My eyes dart to Enzo, flipping a coin, it floats somersaulting in the air.

"Enzo cut it out. You're scaring Abby."

He picks the coin out of the air. "Am I scaring you?"

"No." I shake my head.

"Good. Watching your sister turn will be one hundred times worse."

My heart pounds, I don't even want to picture that. She could never be like that wolf at the party. She's too good. "What happened to the wolf?"

"I killed it." A hint of a smile, Enzo forces the coin to disappear.

"You—What? That was a person! What about prison?"

"So, it could kill everyone there? No."

"There isn't a supernatural prison."

"No. Certain individuals imprison others. It's kidnapping to you humans. There are very few people who can enforce laws and get away with it."

"Like who?"

"The Queen of Hell. Alex, daughter of Lucifer." Enzo answers. "She is the most powerful being in the universe. Don't get on the wrong side of her."

He acts casually, like these are everyday things, to him they are. But it sends my head spinning. Hell is real. Lucifer is real. There is a devil. "Daughter of Lucifer? What happened to him?"

"Alex overthrew him."

"Really how?"

"There are a lot of rumours." Colt puts in.

"So Hell. Heaven. They are real?"

"Not like that, but yes. It's all in the book." Enzo waves absently to my book.

I clutch it. "Thank you."

A shrug, Enzo turns back to the window.

Colt takes my arm, I don't pull away. "We should go. I'll take you to your sister."

"Okay, thank you." My mind is whirling. I can't quite believe it is real.

CHAPTER TWO

Silven

My wings flap, they beat on my back. My head twitches, the extreme heat burning my slimy body. I am in the murky pit called Hell, the embers smoke from the ground. Slowly, my hands slip on my cell bars. I rattle them, howling in anger. They burn my inflamed skin. Lucifer howls in the cage next to mine. How did it get to this? I was second in command. The loyal servant to Lucifer. Lucifer, the King of Hell. All the other demons looked up to me in fear. My every demand would be obeyed. Lucifer would ask me for my service, I was an asset to Hell. I am the strongest of my type of demon alive. Yet, Lucifer got himself overthrown by his dreadful daughter. Leaving Lucifer and I powerless in our own home.

Simply Alex is to blame.

Lucifer's demons haven't tried to save us. Instead, they torture us, at Alex's demand. Long nails wrap around the cage bars. Alex, the little bitch. If only she had stayed dead. A stupid old dead witch resurrected her with more power than she had before. All Lucifer wanted was that power and she stole it to save a couple of humans, her brother and his wife. Pathetic! Lucifer deserved it more.

No-one is loyal to Lucifer, they are loyal to whoever is the most powerful. They will do anything to save themselves. All except me. I would rather be tortured for eternity or killed than to switch sides. My situation is temporary. I plan to get out of Hell and go to Earth. I will find a way for my King to rule once more. Also to seize my revenge and kill Alex. My nails clink on the metal bars. My time will come. The iron door swings open, ready for my daily dose of torture. I don't care. The more time out of my cell, the more time I have to plan my escape. Plotting routes to escape to my well-deserved freedom.

Enzo

I watch Colt get in the car, Abby too. I could magic them a portal. They would be there in an instant, but Colt wouldn't appreciate that. Abby is human and fragile. A portal would make her uneasy. Unlike me, I was born what I am, Colt was turned, like Holly. In my many hundred years of life, no turned human takes it well. Magic flickers from my fingertips. Warlock Hellhound. Hybrids are rare but they happen. Most hybrids are born that way. My mother was a Witch and my father was a Hellhound. Luckily, they were both powerful for their kind, making me equally powerful as both.

Memories of my parents flash in my mind, I shake my head. No. I won't think about them. Relaxing, my glamour falls, goat horns appear on my head. One broken in half, the stub sharp. My eyes glow, fire reflecting in their glow. The eyes of my father, the horns from my mother. Touching the broken horn, I can remember that day vividly, it was the first day I could enjoy the sweet smell of dew in the forest after many years of captivity. I push that thought away too.

I stand abruptly, my magic had taken the body away. I sent the body to a ravine no-one will find it. I thought Abby would be pleased, she wasn't. I don't understand humans. They have the death penalty. They believe in punishment but are horrified when someone actually carries it out. I killed that werewolf fairly. It attacked Colt, I had the choice of Colt or the lone werewolf. I picked Colt. The only unjustifiable murder is that of the innocent. That werewolf wasn't innocent.

Running my hands through my hair, my palm scratches a horn. I use a glamour to hide my goat horns, so humans don't see them. Personally, I don't mind them, nor try to hide them. I used to not bother with a glamour. I don't care what people think. But Colt does. He hates drawing attention or being called a freak. So, I hide them for his sake, when we are in the human's sight. I refused to go to high school with Colt, I've been, I went to college as well. That was centuries ago.

Colt is a young vampire, he was only turned a few years back. That day plays vividly in my head. Colt was so lost, crying, covered in blood, fangs hanging out his mouth. Colt had killed the vampire that killed him. Colt didn't want to be a vampire, but slowly, he's accepting it. I am glad he's come a long way from that poor child I rescued. I know why Colt wants to help them. He was once in their place, he wants to do what I did for him. He wants to give back, also he feels guilty. It was his party. At our home. The party I begrudgingly let him throw so he could connect with the humans.

The door to my bedroom swings open, it's perfectly neat. I don't own many possessions. A bookshelf, full of knowledge. A few weights on a rack, there is a gym downstairs where I do the majority of my exercise. A closet of clothes, a bed and an desk, empty except for a laptop. My adjoining room holds more belongings. Potions, spell books, meditation mat. The room is my escape. Sitting down, I settle on the plain blue mat in my second room. My eyes meet the blank wall and I close my eyes.

Hell's Daughter

Falling, I tumble on the grass. My face is drawn, without emotion.

"Please. Don't kill me. I'll do better. Please."

The begging and pleading before a blast of magic fries a hole in their chest. Dead. Glazing, their eyes colour fades. Shrugging, I turn from the body, leaving. The Paris lights shine in my eyes. The night cold, pulling up my coat to hide the edges of my face, I march along the street. The body left, on the cobble. One hundred years old and powerful. Feared. The clattering of police wagons, with their shrill voices, echo in my head. Currently, I'm upholding my words. 'I will make Hell seem like Heaven in comparison to your life once I'm done with you.' That is what I said to the organisation who took away my family. They killed my parents. They kept me, to experiment on. My age at the time made me unable to fight back. They did it for years. I'm still exacting my revenge. Still making my words a reality. Slipping down the road, I disappear into the crowds of Paris.

I open my eyes, I have many memories from my long life. I was told my memories would fade over time and merge. I am five hundred years old and that hasn't happened yet. I could recite the name of every friend, lover and family member I ever had. I can recall the dates and times of events that happened as if they had happened yesterday. Important events and people stay with you, especially funerals. I've been to a few dozen and to this day I can recall the flowers, how many people buried them, who was there, the lettering on the tombstone there was one. Some are more vivid than others, I visit the graves often, whenever I want to be alone.

Abby

Driving towards the hospital, I clutch the book. The silence growing tense, the road long and empty ahead. Few street-lamps work, fluttering. The house is on the edge of the city, the area is badly kept, a sad sign of the lack of care. The road is bumpy with long frequent cracks, unlike smooth city roads.

"So—I guess you're pretty old, huh?" I try to start a conversation.

Colt looks surprised. The new black pick-up truck ponders along at a gentle pace. "No, actually I'm twenty-one. I stopped ageing at seventeen."

He is right, he doesn't look a day over seventeen. If he tried, a few could believe he was eighteen. Twenty-one? That is young. He hasn't lived over a human lifespan. Despite being a vampire, he is only a few years older than me.

"Enzo is old, he says he's not older than five hundred but I swear he's older."

Enzo seems to be grumpy enough to be five hundred, at least but I don't know much about him. Less than I know about Colt.

"Who is Enzo exactly?"

The man I'd met, he was closed off. He didn't want anything to do with the situation. He was quiet and deadly serious. A murderer. That demon devouring into sparks. I can only imagine what happened to the wolf. I don't understand. How is it any different to murdering a person? Enzo sees a difference. He had said they don't have laws. Then what drives them to be good? Why aren't they taking over the streets, killing one another? There has to be some form of code of conduct.

"Enzo is a hybrid. Warlock and Hellhound. I thought I told you?"

"Yes, I mean who is he? Like your brother? Or—"

"Oh do you mean what's his deal?" Colt's lips quirk in a smile. "Enzo is like a big brother. He found me when I was

Hell's Daughter

turned and taught me. He taught morals, how to keep my humanity."

I highly doubt that. His 'morals' appear to be very farfetched. "Morals? He killed someone."

"He believes guilty people deserve to die. Innocent people should be avenged."

"Do you agree?"

"Not entirely. But everyone has their own opinion and judgement. Enzo is a good person, he is just cold. You would be too if you went through what he did."

"What happened to him?"

"Nothing good. It was horrible, even I don't know all the details. He has refused to tell me."

My mind races, what could be so bad? My sister just got turned into a werewolf.

"Was he turned?"

"No, he was born the way he is."

I frown, my hand opens the leather strands, unknotting them to reveal the ratty pages. The pages are thick, and on a style of paper, I'd never seen before, rough to touch. It's handwritten, cursive writing with dark ink. Not with a normal ballpoint pen. It's calligraphy.

"Jeez- It's old."

Colt chuckles lightly. "It is old, Enzo wrote it in the 1800s."

My jaw drops, this belongs in a museum. Enzo does too. He was alive, before my great, great grandparents. Then it hits. Immortality is real, there are people who live forever without growing a day older. They can physically watch people age, from a baby to an elderly person. It is hard to comprehend.

"Immortality is real? Both of you are immortal?"

"Of course, immortality is real. Enzo is lucky he is. He had the chance he wouldn't be. Hellhounds don't live forever, warlocks do."

"Does that mean you can't be killed?"

"No, we can be. Immortality means we cannot age but we can be killed any other way. Also, vampires can be killed with anything, not just wood. Just like werewolves aren't more affected by a wound caused by silver than any other weapon. That is a myth. Read about it with your sister."

I nod. "Thanks."

He parks, we have reached the hospital. I jump out of the car.

The next few minutes are a blur, all I know is I am by my sister's bedside. I didn't realise how desperate I was to see her until we got to the hospital. Her eyes are open, and she is alive. Apparently, they had to do a transfusion due to the large amount of blood loss and countless stitches. They have given her drugs for the pain.

"Holly," I whisper, nudging her shoulder gently.

"Abby." My sister grins dopily.

"I'm so happy you're alive." I hold her hand.

"So am I."

Her glasses wait on the table, would she need them now? Holly is blind without her glasses, but she doesn't even squint to see me.

"That wolf bit me hard but the doctors said I'm healing fast."

And I know why. I clutch her hand, for my support more than hers. I understood why they told me first, so I could soften the blow. I need to tell her.

"You are healing fast. Because..."

"Are you okay?" Concern enters Holly's voice.

"I should have never brought you to the party." I murmur.

"What? No! I had fun until that moment. Don't blame yourself. I'm fine."

"You aren't fine. A wolf bit you."

I can't believe Holly is the calm one out of us, normally it is the other way around but she doesn't know what I do... I need to tell her, I take a deep breath. "It was a werewolf."

"A werewolf?" Holly frowns then chuckles after. "A new prank, already? I appreciate you trying to cheer me up but..."

"It's true. You're a werewolf." I splutter it out. That probably wasn't the best way to say it, I mentally curse myself. I'm so stupid.

"Look at me." Colt touches her shoulder.

"Who are you?"

Holly goes pale, at his touch. Due to Colt's lack of body heat, he is freezing. She turns the shade of the bedsheet, almost blending in with it. "You—are?"

Colt glances my way, I nod at him supportively. She won't believe us unless she has proof. "I'm a vampire. Don't be scared. See." His eyes glow, fangs pop up, cutting his lower lip.

The two fang teeth are like usual teeth except longer and the points are a lot sharper. They retract in a moment. "We are here to help. I promise."

Immediately Holly screams, the sheer earth-shattering cry painful to my ears. "Get out! Get out!" Holly's shrill voice rings.

Colt's face drops in devastation. This is exactly how he thought I would react. That's why he didn't want to show me his face. "I'm sorry. I..." He's gone out the door, I don't even see him leave.

"Are you okay? That monster—" Holly trails off, pulling me into a tight embrace.

My heart thunders in my chest. Pure horror over her face, she peers over her shoulder to make sure 'the monster' is gone. She is now one of those 'monsters' how do I convince her of that? More importantly, how can I get her to accept herself?

Trinity-Rose Crane

Hell's Daughter

Silven

Howling, my entire body throbs. The soaking lava around my body burns the rubbery flesh. As quickly as I am in, I am taken out. The ice-cold water steaming from my skin. The lava dripping from my body. The mixture cooling and hardening on my skin. Hard rocks forming on my flesh. The lumps attached, weighing my body down. My joints stiffen unable to move, the rocks fusing to my skin keeping my limbs together. Rising from the water, my torturer's key hangs over his neck. The skeleton key, the one for my cell. I will need it for my escape. Indestructible chains hold my wrist, restraining my power. I hold the element of air, I'm the strongest of my kind. My powers are useless being holed up in a cell. Shuddering, my body covers in large boils: layers of demon skin warping and ripping away. Each stone that is taken away pulling away layers of skin. The bubbles left on my flesh, leave grey bloody marks. I will need a weapon to escape. I cannot get out of these chains, Alex made sure of it. The best blacksmith of demon armour crafted the cuffs. That will not stop me. The rocks are ripped away, screaming I gawp in pain.

After my torture, I am thrown back in my cell. Hissing, I snarl like a beast. My guard laughs. Silveira. Once my partner in crime as we led the demons at Lucifer's command. We were the closest demons could get to friends. Now, she punishes me. For Alex, the demon Queen. Alex knew it would hurt that little more if she was the one to torture me. Everyone fears her, following her every demand blindly. She is the most powerful being alive. They have no sense of loyalty. Even for demons. The only thing they know is self-preservation.

"Alex has decided, you've been punished enough. You are to be executed in a week." Silveria announces with no sign of remorse.

My eyes widen. I shall be executed. I guess Alex realises she can't break me. That was her goal. Get the last of Lucifer's army to turn against him. Break his spirit that little more. This does mean my plan must be moved forward. I can do that. My King will be free no matter the cost. Then, I can rule Hell with him. And Earth. Everything will be ours. I laugh while the demon marches down the corridor.

CHAPTER THREE

Enzo

I watch the car pull up on the driveway, it is speeding almost crashing into the garage. I'm glad I didn't let him take the McLaren. That is in the garage, it is my favourite sports car. The pick-up is the vehicle I taught Colt to drive in. He has driven it to high school a few times. He doesn't bother putting it in the garage, he leaves it in front of the house. I sigh, there is a garage for a reason. Marching to the front door he looks distraught. Damn it. I can imagine that it didn't go well. I snap my hand, the truck begins to put itself in the garage.

The front door slams open. "How did she take it?" I ask as my fingers flicker; a meal appears on the table.

"Fine." Colt grumbles.

Colt is not okay. Each time I magic our meals, he always cracks a bad joke about how he only lives with me because he can't cook for himself. Or I can't die otherwise he'd starve to death. I get nothing now. I groan. Here comes the hardest part of my long life. Emotions! I never understood them. Revenge is my limit of emotional intelligence.

"What happened?" I bite into the fried chicken laid in front of me, dipping it in garlic sauce, only just a little.

"Nothing." He stabs the chicken, he has his own blood sauce. It is the only way for him to eat normal food.

"Colt." I hiss, a little anger flaring, I don't accept lies. "Don't lie to me."

Instantly, Colt's head dips. I know that look. Regret.

"I'm sorry."

I nod accepting the apology. Colt has lied to me before, that didn't end well. It caused a bigger problem than if he had just told me the truth. If someone has to lie, they must be able to do it properly. Jemma, my dear friend, died because she lied to me. I would have been able to help her if she had told me what was going on. My eyes bore into Colt's as he cowers. Silence looming.

"She called me a monster." He crumbles under the pressure.

"That little—" I slam down my cutlery. "No that's… I won't allow that." I scowl. Differences don't make us monsters, they make us stronger. Humans just need to trust us. No-one should be ashamed of what they are. They only call us monsters out of fear.

"Colt. I swear—"

"You are not doing anything."

I glare at him, I'd like him to try and stop me. I have boundaries of respect I do not let anyone cross. Especially with Colt. I promised myself I wouldn't let anyone harm him the second I saw him. The skinny, blood-soaked boy in the rain crying, without a home.

"She is in shock. If you go and pick a fight and blow some magic in the air you are only going to confirm her theory."

"I wasn't going to attack her. I just want to talk to her." I defend myself truthfully. I am not stupid. I don't want to scare Holly or get revenge. That will not fix the problem. I want to prove Colt is not a monster. She will transform into a werewolf one day. She needs to accept what she is before it's too late.

"I wouldn't risk scaring her." I promise. "I know you want to help the girl. I wouldn't do anything to jeopardise that."

Colt sinks in his seat, hands holding up his head.

"I want to talk to her that's all."

Colt waves his hand, sending me on my way. I take that as a yes. He bites into his blood pudding.

Turning, I go to leave the room. My plate clears itself from the table. I pause at the doorway, I forgot to ask the dreaded question. "Are you okay?"

"I'll live." His face lightens up at his quirky joke.

I roll my eyes, in secret relief. "One more question, why are you so insistent on helping her? She called you a monster."

"You helped me. I want to help someone else."

I accept the answer. He is right. Newly turned can have problems. Lose control, kill. Or hate themselves, and what they've become, enough to kill themselves. The death rate for newly turned supernaturals is scarily high, the majority of deaths are the result of suicide. Colt is right to help them, personally I wouldn't have told Abby. She took it well luckily. Holly will definitely be more of a struggle. A portal appears before my eyes with a flick of a wrist.

"Don't be gone long, okay?"

"I won't." I fly through.

Abby

I jump a foot in the air. The book drops from my lap, onto the floor. Enzo materialises out of no-where.

"Where did you come from?" My heart beats a million times a minute.

"Portal." He states bluntly.

I eye Enzo, I identify two long bones sticking out the top of his forehead. Horns. He has horns! One is splintered stub, and half the length of the other.

His eyes glow in an off colour, red sparks in them. The black horns match his hair.

"You have horns?" I grin.

Enzo scowls. "Haven't you read the book yet?" It hops back in my lap with a snap of his fingers.

"Is there a way I can become a warlock? Seems like it would be useful." I smile. I would love to be able to summon food, teleport and move objects without having to stand.

Enzo takes a step back, analysing me to see if I am being serious. Not looking amused. My smile fades from my face. Holly sleeps in her bed, face brighter than it usually is. She had been sedated after screaming about monsters. Doctors think it was a nightmare due to the trauma, but I know better. I just want her to sleep, I don't want to face her again. She'll have to accept the truth eventually, she can't hide from it forever.

The book turns pages in my lap, words glistening. I read 'Each Warlock bears an animal feature'. Enzo's horns are a pitch black, beautiful even. They curl slightly, goat horns. They point away from his head. One is cut short, not curling like the other. Enzo has a sharp jawline, high cheekbones to complement that. Wide dazzling fiery eyes, concentrating on my sister. Muscles tense and strain

against the shirt, he must work out. How hadn't I noticed the horns before? Enzo's eyes narrow. Damn it. I was staring, I flicker my eyes back to my sister.

"We can hide our marks with a glamour, but I don't unless humans are around." He examines Holly's sleeping body.

"Why is one cut off?" I have gone too far. Enzo's jaw sets hard, he ignores my question and grabs my sister's wrist. "What are you doing?"

"I'm going to wake her up. Then heal her."

Hell's Daughter

Enzo's horns disappear. A hand goes over her chest, inches away. In awe, I watch. Purple energy pulse through his hand, the strands like ribbons exploding from his fingertips. Holly gasps, eyes opening. The sedative was meant to last hours. It's been ten minutes. Enzo spent three seconds and she is wide awake.

"Oh my god." Holly breathes. "Who are you?"

"I'm Enzo."

"We are friends." I chip in, the name isn't very useful.

Both heads turn, with the same shocked and confused faces, it is almost comical.

"I'm here to heal you." Enzo replies.

His hands rise, she gasps, grabbing the bed. I don't see sparks fly but I can tell something is happening. I clutch her hand. Holly's body relaxes.

"The pain, it's gone." Her finger's scramble to her side, the wound left as only a scar. Impressive.

"Why didn't you heal her before? At the party you let the ambulance take her." I raise the question. Surely, if he can heal her the trip to the hospital was unnecessary.

I receive a deathly glower. "If you don't remember, I was saving your life. Then, when I got to Holly, some silly humans thought they could do better than me. I was able to do a quick spell, or she wouldn't have survived the ambulance ride. And if I recall I'm not the one who called the humans to collect her."

"Oh." A pit of guilt enters my stomach. Enzo has saved both our lives. He's tried his best and I got angry with him. "Sorry. I —"

Enzo loses interest in me, he stares at Holly. "Would you call me a monster?"

Holly shakes her head. "No. I don't know how but you healed me!" She holds her hand by her healed side. "You are an amazing doctor."

Horns appear back on Enzo's head. Holly stifles a yelp.

"Would you call me a monster?" He repeats the question.

"You—" Holly grabs my arm, pulling me from him. "He's one of them. Leave!"

Enzo's expression doesn't change, remaining neutral unlike Colt, whose face fell, dissolving into sadness. I will never forget that face. Colt wasn't shocked, only hurt, like someone had driven a knife in his gut.

"Get away!" Holly screams, bouncing from the bed, going in front of me. She could barely move moments ago. "Go away!"

"I'll go." Enzo says smoothly. "I just have one thing to say."

Holly snaps back. "What?"

"You thanked me for saving your life. You weren't scared of me then. Now, I have horns, you fear me. But what actually changed? I still saved you, I simply appear different. How has anything truly changed?"

My heart drums in my chest. Enzo speaks in anger, venom spitting in every word. The gold flicker in his eyes return. He gives a very convincing point. Though his clenched fist suggests that isn't what he wanted to say. Why didn't he get mad? Why does he care so much? He didn't before. Enzo grabs the handle to leave.

"Don't go." Holly whispers. Enzo lets go of the handle. "You aren't a monster."

"I know." Enzo agrees. "Neither are you."

Holly's eyes spring with tears. "Am I really a werewolf?"

"Yes."

Holly collapses back in her bed. I hold her hand, tears streaming down her face.

"I'll go." Enzo is visibly uncomfortable. You only have to know him for a few minutes to know he isn't the comforting type.

"No." Holy reaches for him.

Enzo back pedals, wrenching his arm away. "What are you doing?"

"I-I want to thank you." Holly looks confused.

Enzo holds his arm away.

"You saved me, you helped me. I'm sorry I ever called you a monster. You are a good person. I was hoping you would stay."

Enzo looks appalled. "I'm not a good person. Colt is. I'm only here because of him. I'd have happily left you. He's the person you wrongfully called a monster when he was trying to save you. Thank him." He snarls. Wrenching the door handle he disappears.

In defeat Holly sits on the bed. "Colt, he is the vampire?"

I nod. "Yeah, that was him."

"I shouldn't have called him a monster."

I shake my head, she shouldn't have. "I'm sure you can make it up to him."

"How are you okay with this?" Holy pulls me onto the bed.

"Because Enzo, the bastard…" I glare at the door, checking he's gone. He treated my sister badly. I don't appreciate it. I was happy when he was keeping the anger in. Holly found out she is a werewolf. Our parents didn't pick up the call from the hospital. There is nothing they could do anyway, not from Italy. Admittedly, she shouldn't have called Colt a monster. She will apologise for that. Currently, Holly needs support, Enzo did not give her that. "…Enzo is right. You haven't changed. You still are Holly. Only you can transform into a badass wolf."

Holly laughs, sniffling a little.

"It will be okay. You'll be fine. I'm here for you, Colt and Enzo."

"What about Selena? What should I tell her?" Luckily, Selena was convinced to go home by Holly and the doctors before I got there.

"We can discuss Selena later." I promise.

Should we tell her? Enzo seems pretty against the idea that I know, let alone another person. What about our parents? I'll ask Colt for advice on that. I have no idea.

"I'm a werewolf." Holly whispers. "Will I change every full moon?"

I scoop up the book. "We need to read this together." I open to the passages about werewolves I'd been reading. Holly curls up, like a child against my arm. "Okay." I start from the beginning, reading slowly, the words are hard to read because of Enzo's handwriting. Holly takes a deep breath, tears in her eyes but they aren't pouring. "Werewolves have the ability to…"

Hell's Daughter

Enzo

Colt marches into my bedroom. I lie in bed, throwing and catching a ball of magic. My hand stops, the ball disappears. I sit up, grabbing my shirt from the chair. "What's up?"

Colt swings in my desk chair. I frown, it's not for spinning. I should never have agreed to let him pick any furniture for the house. He can't resist going around in those chairs like a child. Colt stops the chair quickly, eyes lost. "I'm not a monster, am I?"

I scowl deeply, I shouldn't have let him talk to Holly. I should have known it would lead to nothing good. Colt, unlike me, still hasn't come to grips with the fact that he is not a bad person nor a monster nor a beast, freak of nature and all the other names humans call us. I don't believe that bullshit. Colt does, struggling between believing in himself or other people. Trying to convince him to not listen to them has been hard. Yet, I don't blame him, of course he'd believe the people he'd trusted all his life. Why not trust them when they call him a monster? Like in all the books, that's how they portray vampires to be. They see a difference in someone or something and become afraid. Making them irrational with hatred. Colt hasn't seen that yet. "You aren't a monster." I sigh.

"Holly called me a monster." Colt murmurs. "I drink blood to survive. How am I not a monster?"

"Because you are a good person." I answer with ease because it's the truth.

Colt is a good person. I've killed people. Only guilty people and I don't regret it for a second. I have killed for revenge and worse. They all deserved it. Colt on the other hand is different. I remember the night we had gone out to the forest. I was still training Colt to control himself. He disappeared, I found him immediately. Vampires have super-speed but so do Hellhounds. Colt was devouring a fox, saving an innocent rabbit from attack. Colt bit the fox to save the poor defenceless creature. I was proud of him. He fed on the guilty fox, not the innocent rabbit, though it would have been an easier kill. I didn't expect what was to happen next. I remember the warm breeze, as Colt began to tremble. Begging me to save the not-yet-dead fox. He hated what he had done. I did save the fox. Rufus lives in our garden. Colt didn't want Rufus harming any more animals. I feed him to prevent that. My food is formed by magic, not by killing animals.

"Colt, being a good person isn't what you are but what you do. If you believe you are doing good, then you are probably doing the right thing."

Colt smiles again. "You say that every time."

"It's the truth." I shrug, hopefully I won't have to repeat it again.

"Thanks." Colt puts out a fist.

I raise my eyebrow, something he's learnt at school no doubt. "Seriously?"

"Come on. Please." I put out my fist, knocking our fists together. In a 'fist bump'. I don't understand it. I'm better at magic messages than this modern thing.

Colt grins triumphantly. "You did it."

"I'm not doing it again." I protest.

"You can't leave me hanging." He argues.

My eyebrows shoot up. "What?"

Colt sighs. "You can't not do it. Otherwise you leave me hanging."

I roll my eyes. "I will 'leave you hanging' next time." I quote him.

Colt laughs, it doesn't sound forced either. I listen carefully to the notes. I check my watch, it's one o'clock in the morning.

"Aren't you going to bed before school?"

"Nah." He does one grand spin on the chair.

I don't blame him, he's always more awake at night. He is a vampire. The chain on his wrist glistens in the lamp light, it has an enchantment to let him walk in the sunlight. Only ten exist in the world. Only ancestry magic can make them, no warlock understands how it works there isn't a book. I have experimented on it, but even I can't understand how it works enough to make more. The plain chain wraps around his wrist gracefully, I remember his face when I gave it to him. It had been two months since I'd found him. I had to trust him before I gifted it to him, that chain is very powerful. Colt's entire face lit up like a bonfire. He hugged me, so tightly I thought my lungs would collapse. We spent that morning watching the sunrise on the roof of my house. I have never seen Colt so happy.

I've never told him how I got in possession of it, he has never asked. Margherita, my old vampire friend from long ago had one of the ten. Margherita died in my arms, her frilly blue dress soaked in blood from the arrow through her heart. It was the day before she was going to marry the love of her life. I tried to save her, but she was gone before my magic could heal her. I found the bracelet around my wrist later. I hadn't realised she put it there before she died. Robert, the groom to be, a mortal, killed himself at the news. I buried them together. They didn't receive a proper burial. No-one could ever see Margherita's body, shrivelled, pale, fang teeth out, black veins scarring the skin. If people had seen that, they would have hung her in the town square, to be spat on, then burned. They would have been dancing on her grave instead of crying. I would never have allowed that. They are buried deep in a forest in Italy. Margherita and Robert did nothing to deserve what happened to them. I killed the people who killed them, enjoying every second of it. Revenge, Margherita said, was always one of my talents. I shake my head, falling out of the memory.

"Neither of us will sleep." I stand. "I'm going for a jog."

Colt nods. "I have homework, you wouldn't happen to know what trigonometry is, would you?"

"What?" I scrunch my nose. "What stupid things are they filling your head with now?"

Colt laughs. "This is the simple stuff." He pulls the page out of his pocket.

I stare at the array of triangles on the paper, scattered with numbers and letters to form equations. "I've lived for over five hundred years and I have never needed that before, or ever seen it."

Colt chuckles. "I also have an essay due in the morning."

"I'm not magically doing your homework again."

"Fine." Colt snatches the pages out of my hands. "I'll do it now."

I grab my hoodie. "I'll be back soon."

Colt nods. "You will help me with next week's homework, right?"

I roll my eyes. "What is it?"

"A book review on a novel called Margherita's Escape. It is for history, it's meant to have an accurate representation about what happened in the nineteen hundreds."

I know the name of that book. I wrote it. I've written many books. It's been my most popular job ever. I write when I feel like using a pseudonym. "Fine. I'll be back soon."

My feet pound on the driveway, one thing I do not miss from the past is the shoes and clothes. The frilly shirts, posh jackets, tall hats and uncomfortable shoes. I stick the headphones in my ears and pound down the streets. The music of this generation is good but I have heard much better.

Abby

The day at school was quiet. I didn't get to talk to Colt. He's not in any of my lessons today. Holly spent the day dodging people or staring at her hands as if they would magically start changing before her eyes. I continue to soak in the information from the book. I read it during break and lunch trying to remember every detail. I understand all the passages about

Hell's Daughter

Werewolves, Hellhounds, Warlocks and Vampires. I have learnt so much about the supernatural that my head wants to explode.

I didn't sleep a wink last night. Holly returned home and our parents don't know about the incident, Holly wants to keep it that way. I don't blame her. It would be hard to explain. I've been checking on her all day. Werewolves can transform under any sort of pressure or stress unless they learn how to control it. I tried to convince her to take the day off. She refused. Colt has promised to help, but will he after what she said? I wouldn't blame him if he changed his mind.

My phone buzzes while we walk out the gates after a successful day with no drama. I check the message, Kyle, asking to meet up. I curse. I'd hoped it would be Colt. I haven't spoken to him all day. I reply to Kyle with a polite 'no'.

"Holly?" Selena calls behind us.

Holly's eyes widen, to the size of balloons in panic. "No. I can't—" Holly has been avoiding Selena all day and hasn't replied to her messages since yesterday evening.

"It's okay, we'll say hello and leave." I try to relax her.

Holly gulps but doesn't try to run.

"Hi, Selena." I grin.

"I can't believe you're up! It's incredible. You really scared me yesterday!" Selena jumps in and pecks her cheek.

"Yeah..." Holly looks at me for help.

"It wasn't as bad as it looked but Holly needs to rest. She'll call you later."

I grab Holly's arm protectively, pulling her along in a hurry. Selena watches, in confusion, luckily, she doesn't follow.

Holly breathes, "Thanks."

I look at her hands, they unclench. The palm of her left hand bleeds with a puncture wound. Stress, Holly hadn't seemed to notice.

"Where are you going?" A gruff, permanently annoyed voice rings behind us. Enzo strides in our direction, Colt close by.

I relax. "Hi."

"Where are you going?" Enzo demands again.

"Home." Holly answers.

He shakes his head. "Didn't you get my message?"

"No. Wait. You have my number?" I don't remember giving that to him.

"Enzo, did you send a message using magic again?" Colt sighs.

"Yes." Enzo snorts, like it was obvious.

"Did any paper fly at you today?" Colt asks.

I recall the day. At lunch, I got hit on the head with a paper airplane. I yelled at the people sitting behind us, for hitting me with it. "Yeah, I instantly threw it in the trash."

Holly nods. "Same. I got hit in History."

Enzo rolls his eyes heavily, I could practically hear him say 'you're so stupid'. "Next time, read the paper."

Colt smiles at me, teeth glinting. Then, something in my mind clicks. Remembering a passage from the book, vampires can't stand in the sun. "How are you outside? It's daylight."

"I have..."

"No." Enzo cuts him off. "We need to go."

"Where?" Holly frowns.

I really see it then. Enzo rubs his temple. He looks ready to slap some sense into us using magic. Acting like we are stupid, an irritating leech he can't shake. Somehow the answer should be obvious.

"We need to help Holly, she is dangerous till she can control her changes. We plan to teach her." Colt explains, reasonably.

"I mean the fact you even dared go to school is shocking. What if you'd changed?" Enzo boots crumple the leaves under them. "Come on."

He waves his hand for us to follow into a small alley.

Once we get there, a swirl of colour appears, the glow is beautiful. It is a perfect circle, arrayed in a sea of purple and sky blues with twinkling lights.

Hell's Daughter

"It is a portal." Enzo adds.

"You may feel a bit nauseous." Colt warns.

I nod, the swirling liquid absorbing Enzo with it. I hold my breath. Holly grabs my arm, and we step forward. Bracing myself, Holly melts away from me. My head spins, colour flashing before my eyes, legs gliding on nothing. Jolting, my feet leave the ground. The world tilts sideways. I feel no sense of reality or direction. A ringing noise, and blue flashing lights. Suddenly I'm released on the other side. Holly stumbles. I clutch her for support.

"Are you okay?" Enzo's voice drips with sarcasm.

I scowl, straightening my posture. "Yes."

Looking around, we are deep in a forest. The trees are thick, the trunks triple the size of any I've seen before. The oak, dark with grooves that show age. Trees here haven't been touched in centuries. The bushy leaves, a dark luscious green from large amounts of sunlight and little pollution. We are in a small clearing, around us you can't see any further than twenty metres ahead. The tree roots growing above the dirt, overlapping one another. No-one could go far in without falling over. There are no paths, foot made or otherwise. It's completely deserted. The sun radiates on my skin. Birds chirp in my ears. They are completely out of tune. Honestly, it is terrible, birds have never sounded so bad. Worse than when they wake you up in the morning. I've never seen this forest before.

Holly takes a deep breath.

"Are you okay?" My question is genuine unlike Enzo.

"The birds are so darn annoying." Her eyes begin to gleam a yellow tint.

I chuckle. "I know."

"Colt, tell them how it works." Enzo orders, sitting on a rock, long coat flapping around him. Colt smiles, ignoring Enzo, who glares.

"Basically, your first transformation will be the most painful. We must trigger it, feed emotions which cause you to change. I won't lie, you'll never have worse pain."

Holly becomes tense, her nails digging into my arm, hard enough to draw blood. My heart pounds, I wish it was me. Holly doesn't deserve this. I wish I could take it away for her, even if I have to have it myself. As long as she was okay.

"After you change, so will Enzo. He'll take you through using your senses, walking, running and turning back."

Holly nods. "I'm-- really changing?" Panic enters her voice. "I won't hurt anyone will I?"

"No. That's what Enzo is for."

Holly bites her lip, enough for it to bleed.

"Just a warning, your clothes will rip to shreds. Enzo can magic you new ones."

"I'll be here the entire time." I promise.

Holly smiles reassuringly at me. "Thanks."

I can see the fear in her eyes. Her arms wrap around me, trembling. No matter how much she tries to hide it.

"You can't follow her when she is a wolf. You'll never keep up." Enzo shucks his coat, leaving it folded neatly on the rock.

Holly nods slowly.

"We must trigger the transformation. What makes you mad?" Colt asks.

Holly frowns. "I'm not sure. The birds are kind of annoying."

"Anything else?"

Holly looks bewildered, Enzo looming over her for answers. Colt is calm, but that doesn't help much. Hopefully, Enzo's a nicer hound than human. Otherwise, Holly isn't going to be able to cope. I haven't known him very long but it's easy to tell he's not a warm person.

"I-I don't know." Holly stutters.

"Fine." Enzo rolls his eyes. "We can work with birds."

Colt scowls. "Not too much."

He nods. They share a look, I frown in confusion about what is going on. Holly doubles over in pain, eyes widening. Enzo clamps his hands to her head. Holly's full body weight lands on me. Her legs giving out with horrific snaps. I lower her to the ground. Tears stream down her face.

"Shut up!" She screams.

"Get off her." I demand.

Enzo doesn't seem to register her reaction, while sending my sister in pain. Absolute fear enters her eyes, causing dread to pump through my veins.

"Get off her!" I shove him, he doesn't move, remaining as still as a rock. "What are you doing?"

"I'm amplifying the bird noises while manipulating what she sees. Till she is angry enough to transform completely. Incomplete transformations are more painful."

I bite my lip, what should I do? Beg him to stop? Or let him. "How bad is it?"

"I can show you." Enzo offers a beaming hand.

"No!" Colt interrupts. "Abby is not doing that."

"It's a drop compared to Holly's amount." Enzo waves a powerful finger.

I accept. My world goes to darkness. My ears ring. Birds, the awful croaking noise, kill my ears, causing them to bleed. I want to rip them off my head. I feel beaks peck all over my body. I stumble around pointlessly. Unable to do anything. They swoop biting my skin. I have no power. I'm useless as they take over. Forcing me to squirm, I swat the angry birds but they keep returning. A hurricane of swirling birds forms around me. Furious, I howl. My eardrums ready to burst and blood pumping so hard I can feel it through my entire body.

"Enzo!" Colt hisses over the horrific noise.

My eyes open, and I collapse feeling weak and dizzy. A smug look crosses Enzo's face. I can still hear them. Mocking me. I stop as an echoing crack vibrates through the forest. A whimper. "Help me."

Holly is in a ball on the ground. Fur on her palms, thick and coarse. Yellow eyes glow instead of her natural brown ones. Spasming her entire body seizes, I can see the muscles move under her skin. They slither and stretch moving around the bones. Holly gasps for air, claws wrapping around my wrist. Fear fills Holly's eyes, tears dripping down her cheeks. A scream rips from her throat, one that makes my own chest hurt.

"Holly, it'll be okay. You can do it." I try to support her.

She shakes her head, heavily. "Everything." She wheezes. "Every-everything-" She can't finish the sentence.

Bones crack over her next words, she lets go of my hand. Clothes rip to shreds. Her mouth full of spit frothing around her lips. Thick coarse blonde fur sprouts out of her skin. More bones click out of place. I feel my stomach churn, trying not to throw up at the sickening noise. The scream turns into a howl of sheer pain. My heart beats faster, wishing to take her place, or at least relieve some of her pain. Holly lies on the ground, howling in agony, like it is burning all over.

"Help her. Please. There must be something you can do." I spin to Enzo and Colt.

"No." Enzo shrugs, carelessly.

"Please! Anything!"

Colt hesitates, thinking.

"No." Enzo glares at him.

I catch the glance. "You can do something! Please. Do it!"

"If I ease her pain now, she won't be able to deal with the pain later." Enzo explains.

I pause. I want to help. I really do. But Enzo knows more about this. I want the pain to go but she will be better off if I leave it. It's not my decision, but Holly's and she can't respond. A wolf howl echoes cutting off my thoughts. Spinning a bewildered wolf face greets me. The strong stench of vomit from the bushes.

"Holly?" I croak, heart pounding in worry.

Hell's Daughter

She stumbles back shaking her head. The wolf, blonde, larger than Holly, a scared look in her eyes. The wolf is beautiful. The only other one I have seen tried to kill me so I didn't have much time to admire it. Breathtaking, my sister turned into an actual wolf.

"Hi." I smile.

A bark, then another. I chuckle in sheer amazement. I don't understand a word she says. Holly collapses onto my lap in exhaustion, head thwacking my thighs. Slowly, I stroke her fur. She goes into the embrace. A howl behind me, I stumble back or I would have if I didn't have a heavy wolf sitting on me. My jaw drops in awe. The hound has black fur, eyes orange with fire. Looking directly in its eyes I can almost see a fiery burning pit. Heat radiates from the animal. It is much larger and stronger than a wolf. A Hellhound. Fire seems to glimpse around the creature, in a wave of pulsing energy. Enzo.

Silven

I grab my bars and shake them uselessly. They are too strong. No demon can get out. I trace them for any cracks or weak points. Not for myself, but for the guard. Once I have that key, I can lock my guard inside and escape. I need to make sure he can't escape, I need every second. My daily gruel arrives, the grey sludge of live hell worms crawls along the plate. I snatch it up. Gobbling the worms I give them no chance to run away. They are ground to a slimy mush by my razor teeth. The fowl taste sticking in my mouth even after I consume them. I need flesh, the meat with blood dripping down my chin. What I would do for solid food, not hell worms. It won't be long. Then I can raise Lucifer. First, I need to find the warlock who cast Lucifer to Hell for eternity. I need him for the ritual, after the human sacrifices.

Taking the plate, I smash it to pieces. I suppose Alex's fortress isn't indestructible after all. Scooping up a handful of shards, my thick skin is tough enough it won't cut. I hold the largest shard.

"Hey!" The guard hisses.

I dart forward, pouncing the piece goes through the skin. He is a thin skinned demon, not a very powerful demon either. Alex underestimated my will and strength. The spear stabs my arm through the bars. It enters as quickly as it is gone. A whisk of his hand, the wind carries the shards away. I hold my one tightly, against the force.

"That's it. I'm tripling your torture tomorrow! No food either!"

I shrug disappearing to the back of my cage. I have what I need.

Grasping the shard, I clutch it, demon blood dripping from it. My wound aches no more. I can endure pain. I've learned to. Every demon does, you don't get far otherwise. We know not to be weak. Dabbing my blood on the shard, I hold it tightly. Beginning my ritual, humming quietly to myself. I call upon the power of Hell. The blood I wield is just enough. The shackles prevent my powers but luckily nothing can stop the will of Hell. So, that is what I use. The shard lights up then fades out. It's done. That poor hunter won't know what hit him. I call on all my power to control the hunter on earth. I need a vessel to stay in to remain on earth and project my being into the human form to finish the job to bring Lucifer back. Sadly, I can't control the hunter from here to do the sacrifices for me, that would need a lot more blood from my guard. I sent the hunter to catch someone close to Enzo Thornhill. Hunters are strong and easy to control, making them perfect for the job. I need Enzo because he is the one who put up the spell. I need his blood to release Lucifer from it. He is of Hell blood and of magic. I hope the hunter chooses a convenient vessel for me to enter while on earth. Hopefully, they'll be ready when I rise. Two days from now.

CHAPTER FOUR

Enzo

I change into a hound, body shifting easily. The pain is no better, but it is ten times quicker, making it bearable. In a minute, I'm on all fours. Holly, in her small timid wolf form in front of me is lying on Abby's lap. Honestly, I'm surprised Abby has lasted this long. I expected her to run and ditch her sister right at the start. Or to run away in fright at the sight of her sister. Human, Holly is timid and small but she has transformed into a beast with teeth sharp enough to grind Abby to pieces. My paws are bigger than her face, perfectly adapted for the rocky mountainous landscape of Hell. Anyone else would have run to the end of the earth and not looked back. I have seen that happen before, more times than I can count. To my ultimate amazement, Abby smiles in my direction. My stern expression falters in surprise, I regain my composure immediately.

Holly strains to her feet, bewilderment in her eyes. I growl softly, communicating with 'Are you okay?'. I remember my first time, it was indescribably painful. I thought I was dying, I knew it would be painful but never that bad. Your entire body aches afterwards, you want to collapse and never get back up. Holly begrudgingly stands up from the safety of Abby's lap. I strain my head in the direction we'll be heading.

"Take care of her." Abby becomes serious, an expression I have never seen on her face before.

I nod, she wouldn't understand anything else.

"I mean it." Abby glares my way as if she has the upper hand.

I reach her shoulder, on all fours and am made of muscle and fire. Mentally, I give her a tick in my good books. I like to judge people that way. Abby isn't just the party girl, I thought she was. I'm almost glad I saved her from drowning. Holly, she is harder. I don't trust her, at all. Not after how she reacted. I have eternity to hold grudges. Colt really owes me for this. Holly's head drops, noticing my movement of annoyance. I bark, the harsh growl deep enough that the birds fly away in squawks of fear. I jerk my head towards the forest.

Feet pounding the forest flies by in an array of beautiful colours. The different shades of green flash merging to one. The trees are gone as soon as they are there, the grass tickles my paws, soft and gentle. I hear the quiet patter of rabbits and mice in the distance. The sweet smell of dew is overwhelming. All our senses get extremely heightened when we transform. The sunlight hits my fur, the heat in my body burning with an equal amount of intensity. Glancing back, Holly is close behind, tongue out enjoying life. I dart between trees, paws up on the roots at the sharp turn. I duck and then slide under a few low branches. My nose goes up to the smell of a herd of rabbits nearby. I spin for them. Holly's wolf face lights up, no longer frightened. The rabbits are getting close, time for her first lesson. Control your urges to eat them all in a murderous rage. Stopping, Holly tries to copy. Skidding past, she thumps in a tree. I chuckle silently. I hoped that might happen. I can't wait for her to try and walk backwards. These things always happen to the newbies.

Hell's Daughter

Abby

Enzo and Holly dart off without a goodbye. Holly doesn't even look back. She is gone after Enzo in a flash. He better take care of her. I will be furious otherwise and he'll have to suffer my wrath. Not that I could do much before those magical hands start flying.

"She'll be okay." Colt's hand goes on my shoulder.

"Yeah?" My voice raises to a question unintentionally.

"Enzo is good, even if he isn't a people person." Colt tugs me onto the grass.

Sighing, I sit on the grass. Colt leans on a tree, staring up at the sky, letting the sun bathe his face.

Colt's skin is tan, unlike the vampires in the movies. He happily relaxes in the sun without a problem, but in the book, it said vampires couldn't go in sunlight. It stated that vampires could last fifteen minutes in the sun before becoming toast.

"How come you are in the sun? Enzo seemed keen to keep it secret." I question Colt, Enzo isn't here to stop him this time.

Colt puts out a wrist, around it is a silver chain.

"That?" I lean close, taking his arm to examine it. "That's it?"

"Did you want an exciting story?" Colt chuckles.

"How does it work?" I touch it gently in awe. I mean what was I expecting an invisible umbrella?

"An enchantment, an old warlock did it. No-one knows how. There are only ten in the world."

My eyes widen, now that is interesting. Ten in the world, ten vampires can walk in the sun.

"Why didn't Enzo want me to know?" I ask.

"He doesn't trust you." Colt answers honestly. "Don't take it personally."

My shoulders droop, I guess I understand that. The bracelet must be worth millions, or more. I can imagine all vampires want to enjoy the day. I can't imagine being stuck inside for twelve hours a day, unable to open the curtains. Hearing the world go on around you while you are stuck inside only coming out when the moon is lit. Living life as a shadow. That would be awful.

"I trust you. Besides, Enzo spelled it. It will never come off, it'll stun anyone who touches it."

I let go of his arm gently. "Enzo must really care about you." I tilt my head and rest it on his shoulder.

"He does, he's like a big brother to me." Colt relaxes. "I wouldn't be who I am without him. I'm glad he found me."

"How did you meet?" I ask.

"I'd just got turned. Enzo appeared just as I had killed the vampire who turned me. I thought I was a monster. I didn't think I deserved to live." Colt's hand turns into a fist. "Enzo took me in, taught me everything, even how to control myself and gifted me the power to walk in the sun."

Colt strokes the silver with a finger.

"That's why you want to help Holly." I connect the dots.

"Yes. Enzo was there for me, I want to be there for someone else."

"What was Enzo doing there when he found you?"

A shrug. "I never asked." Colt spins the chain on his wrist thoughtfully.

"That must have cost a great deal. It must be worth millions."

"It's worth billions." Colt corrects my estimate. "Enzo didn't buy it. He was wearing it when I met him."

I frown. Why would he be wearing a sunlight bracelet? "He's not a vampire."

"So?" Colt doesn't understand where my confusion is coming from.

I sigh, I'm overthinking it. Enzo owned it, so what. He had no-one to give it to. I mean he wouldn't be foolish enough to leave it somewhere. Not with it's worth. I still wonder how Enzo knew Colt was there. And why he helped Colt but didn't want to

Hell's Daughter

help Holly. Colt begged him. Colt obviously doesn't seem to ask many questions about Enzo's life. Yet, there must be something special about Colt. If Enzo was willing to help him.

A cold breeze hits, sending a shiver down my spine. It may be summer, but the wind can still be bitter in the afternoon.

"Want my jacket?" Colt offers, already pulling it off.

"No." I protest.

"I don't feel the cold. I'm a vampire." He reminds me. "Take it."

"Thanks." His hand touches mine in the exchange, it's like putting your hand in the freezer. I shiver in an unconscious reaction. There is no warmth to him at all.

"Sorry." He retracts, dropping the jacket.

"It's fine. Sorry." I wrap the jacket around my shoulders, I lean on him, touching his hand reassuringly.

I didn't mean to shiver, it wasn't in disgust, I needed him to know that. "What do you think they are doing now?"

"Enzo will be teaching her to hunt and not to kill everything in sight." I receive a half-smile. "We can go back if you want, they will be a while."

"No. It's okay." I watch the sun, it is already drooping ready for sunset.

We drift off into silence, both gazing up at the sky. A few long thin clouds drift by in the setting sun.

"Tomorrow, I'm teaching Holly to control changing when she is angry," Colt explains, filling the silence.

"I hope your techniques are better than Enzo's." I chuckle.

"Sorry about him again."

"Don't be, he's doing it not you. What happened to him? I mean, what made him so cold?"

"His life. From the small snippets, I have heard. It wasn't great."

"It can't have been that bad, he has magic and is a badass Hellhound. He didn't have to go through being changed, he was born who he was."

"It's not that simple." Colt's arm goes around me.

I sigh, the grooves of the tree digging in my back. "What about your life? Tell me about it."

A laugh. "What do you want to know? My life is pretty normal."

"That is a lie if I ever heard one. You got turned into a vampire."

"Well until then." A quirk of a real smile.

"Tell me." I relax in his arms feeling safe, encouraging him.

"Fine, if you want to know." Colt falls back in the tree. "Where do I start? Okay, I was in school. My English teacher was new, she wanted to speak to me."

Colt explains. "I thought it was my lack of work or something. I was never the brightest or the most well-behaved. Anyway, I went." A short harsh laugh, nothing amusing about it. "I got there, with a few other of my classmates. Georgie, Sam, Kim and Hetty."

All his muscles tense. "She had put gas in the room, we all went out like lightbulbs. I was first to wake up, she had put us in a warehouse." Listening, I could hear the pain in his voice. "Turns out she was a vampire who pretended to be a teacher, she would get a group of kids, kill or turn them. Then she would move on. She was a serial killer, the police had been chasing her for months."

A deep breath and he continues. "She told me she was going to test us. A survival of the fittest situation. The winner got to join her cult. I ran." His breath hitches. "She caught up instantly, being a vampire, it took her a few seconds. I fought her. I lasted ten minutes but once her teeth sunk in that was it. I had lost. She drank. I woke up a vampire, blood on my hands. I'd killed her in a blind rage. And there was Enzo. The rest of the students were fine. Enzo used his magic to make them forget and go home." Colt's hands are in fists.

"And you. Were a vampire. Alone. That must have felt terrible."

"It did. I felt stupid. All the signs were there, I never saw my teacher arrive or leave school, the blinds were always closed, she didn't patrol the corridors like the other teachers." He curses. "But I had Enzo. He made the transition easier. He told me I saved all the kids there. I was a hero. I want to believe him."

"You did. She would have done the same to them if it weren't for you." I don't agree with murder, but it was self-defence.

"She is the only person I ever killed." Colt relaxes as the story ends. "I moved in with Enzo. Now I'm here."

"What about your family?"

A sharp poisonous laugh to hide the pain. "I was stupid, I told them. They tried to kill me. Enzo made them forget. Took me in. I haven't looked back since. Holly is lucky to have you."

"I'm sorry." I hug him.

"It's okay. I think I told you about Holly's condition first because I wanted her to have someone." A deep breath. "That is why I like you. You freaked out less than Holly did."

"I wish it was me." I answer honestly.

"You do?" Colt moves back in surprise.

"Yes. Holly doesn't deserve this, I would happily take her place to remove her pain."

"You are a good person." Colt smiles.

"What about you? If you could make it another student in your English class, would you?"

Colt's eyes narrow. "I'd never thought about it. I guess at that moment I would have. But now, I wouldn't."

"Why not?" I frown.

"I love my life now, I wouldn't trade it for anything. I would never have met Enzo, I wouldn't be here." Colt waves to the forest. "I didn't think I would like my life now but I do. It's my life. I wouldn't change it for anything."

"Do you think Holly will feel like that? Ever?" I hope.

"Yes, in time."

My shoulders relax, we fall silent. My heart pounds, the noise loud and clear next to Colt. My head by his chest, I don't hear anything from it. No blood pumps through his veins. I pray Holly is doing okay. I wish I could be with her. But I can't.

Colt smiles, "You know we still have an hour or two till they'll return. How about we have some fun, too?"

"What do you mean?" I ask.

"I may not be able to transform into a wolf or make magic fly from my fingers but I'm not useless."

"I read that you have speed and strength." I try to remember the book, there are many pages on vampires. It's hard to remember all the facts.

"Yeah, also night vision, immortality and charming good looks."

I laugh. "Anything else?"

"Our reflexes are great, due to our speed."

"Uh-huh." My hand eases for a pebble on the ground.

"Come on. I promise you'll have fun. Unless you're scared." His eyes twinkle.

The pebbles soar from my hand, heading straight for his face. It lands in his palm a few inches from where I'd thrown it.

"How?" My jaw drops.

"I've dodged a bullet before, I can dodge a pebble."

"A bullet?" How did he dodge a bullet? They travel at one thousand seven hundred miles an hour. "How far away were you?"

"About ten metres away. It was a swift dodge, I know. It wouldn't have been that bad if it hit me. I heal quickly."

"How fast?" I ask, curiously.

Colt takes a jagged rock, cutting his hand. To my surprise it bleeds, I stare at the deep gash. Slowly, I can see it fixing itself. The sides of the skin pinching together. A cut that would need stitches, taking months to heal, had already pieced together. Fading in his hand it takes five minutes and the wound looks a month old and had medical attention.

"That is incredible. How long does it take for a bullet wound?"

"I've never been hit with a bullet yet, I couldn't tell you."

"That's a good thing."

"It is. An arrow hurts like hell. Takes twelve minutes."

"You got hit by an arrow?" I exclaim. I wouldn't expect that, who uses a bow and arrow?

"Enzo is very skilled with a bow and arrow. He prefers it over a gun. He can use magic on arrows. And he was around when they were popular and guns weren't a thing." He quirks a smile.

"Enzo did it?" That shocks me more than that he got hit with an arrow. Colt calls him a brother. Why would he attack him? And why would Colt forgive him?

"Yes. I was learning to dodge incoming objects. Enzo could still hit me if he wanted to. He purposely did clumsy shots back then and they still hit me."

I chuckle, it was a teaching method. Sounds more like Enzo. "You learnt to have good reflexes, huh?"

"Yes. Good thing too or that pebble would have had my eye."

I laugh, Colt puts out his hand. "Come on. Let me show you what I can do."

I stand, taking his hand. "Okay."

"Get on my back." He orders.

"What?"

"Your legs would fall off trying to keep up if I ran holding your hand. Come on."

"Are you sure?" I ask. I'm not heavy but Colt looks very lean. I don't want to hurt him.

Colt sighs, scooping me up in his arms with one swift gesture. I squeal in surprise. I wrap an arm around the back of his neck. "I'm not too heavy, am I?"

"Vampire strength remember."

I tighten my grip around his neck. "I'm not strangling you, am I?"

"I don't need to breathe. Stop panicking." Colt smiles. "Are you ready?"

I nod. "Yeah."

Hell's Daughter

Enzo

I sigh, I swear this is how I'll die. Colt was never this hard to train, though I did want to train him. Maybe that made it more bearable, Holly prances around barely able to stand on her four legs. I show her, again. My feet move slowly. I might as well not be moving. Her furry brows furrow in concentration. I finish three steps and spin a turn. Holly tries again, falling against her chin. How come she could run all the way here? It has been thirty minutes and she has spent more time on the ground than standing. I think… exactly. She wasn't thinking. She ran by instinct last time. I guess I could give it a go. Nothing else is working.

"Run," I order her. "Don't think."

She starts, getting five metres then falling.

"I can't help it." Holly protests in a bark.

Or I think she does. Her dog language is nothing short of abysmal. Exactly how I'd expect a drunk wolf to sound. The words are off, slurring together. I would feel sorry for any human who could hear her. The awful song of yapping instead of a long steady howl. The noise is painful to hear, sadly she has to talk for us to communicate.

I sigh heavily. Colt and Abby are going to kill me for what I am about to do. Shuddering, my entire body bursts into flames, flames large enough to form a bonfire. The flames could burn the entire forest if I let them. My black fur is barely distinguishable under the fire. I howl, turning it to a harsh growl. Holly whimpers cowering a little. Snarling, I charge. As I expected she runs. Without thinking she runs. She is off. Running like her life depends on it. She doesn't fall. As elegant as any wolf, she darts through trees, barely touching the ground. I knew she could do it. She just overthinks every move she makes. In terror, all common sense goes out the window and she reacts.

Trinity-Rose Crane

Hell's Daughter

I stop, the fire dies out on my back. We have gone over a mile. Holly keeps running, yapping madly. I sigh, the ball of fur disappearing in the dark. I continue, looking onward for a minute. I don't want to, but I should get her. Holly doesn't know the woods, she'll get lost. Then that will be pinned on me. I pick up speed, feet pounding, the sound drumming through my body in perfect rhythm. Holly appears quickly enough, she isn't that fast. I just need to get in front of her. I hear a scream echo in the forest. A human, I recognise who it is. Abby. Shit. Launching myself at full speed, I rush to see what trouble Holly has gotten herself into now.

Laughter echoes in the air. I reach the scene in a second. Abby is on the ground, hair a mess and laughing. A lump forming on her forehead. Colt kneels by her side, looking at it. Holly nuzzles her.

Colt smiles. "I think you lost your student."

Holly yaps, seeing me and scampers behind them. She desperately needs to improve her reaction time and how to use her senses. She should have been able to hear me coming. That's what they are there for. To know when a threat is coming. I'll talk to her later so Colt and Abby don't have to hear her yap. I'm not that cruel.

"That's it for today," I tell Holly. I should probably do more with her, but I may go insane. Colt gets her tomorrow. That'll be when he realises what a bad idea this is.

Cautiously, she peeps around from behind Abby's legs. A massive sigh of relief. "How do I change back?" Holly growls.

"Think about it. Imagine yourself changing back and it should happen. Do it in the bushes." I demand.

Holly nods and disappears her eyes on me till the last possible moment. I guess our session is over.

I turn back to the two still on the ground.

"She might need some magical attention." Colt gestures to Abby.

Abby has bruises forming on her arms, most likely her legs too. The bump on her head is growing. Both her eyes dilate slightly.

She giggles. "I think he wants to know what happened."

"We got bored. We were running at vampire speed. Holly came out of nowhere and scared us. I stopped so fast, Abby flew out of my arms and into a tree." Colt explains.

I roll my eyes, the lengths Colt will go to for someone he likes. Two years ago, he kicked me out of my own home for a romantic dinner with some boy. Colt made a cake, with peanuts. The boy was allergic and I had to save him. Colt was in a panic when he called me to help. I won't make fun of him, this time. Well, I might later. Colt would never try and impress a crush with his abilities. He worries they'll scare his love interest away. Or worse they'd call him a monster. At least he can be himself with someone other than me.

"You should go change." Colt suggests.

A bone snaps in the bush, Holly. "I'll go help." Abby stands, stumbling.

"Holly is going to need you to magic her some clothes." Colt waves for me to go in the thick trees. I huff. Colt laughs.

Wandering in the bush I change back into a human. It's easy with practice. I honestly thought I would die during my first transformation. I got over it quickly enough. Holly will too. One day. Though I think it will take much longer for her to come around to it. My fingers flicker, clothes appearing before me, they will for Holly too. I grab the jeans, pulling them on. I tie them up with a belt. It clicks shut, the bushes rustle. Glancing up, Abby stands there.

"Oh my god! I'm sorry. Colt said you'd be done." She doesn't move.

"Could have called out. What do you want?" I sigh and grab my sweater.

Abby blushes, her eyes are still dilated from smacking the tree but they stare at my chest right enough. "Oh… I wanted magical assistance for my head. It is throbbing." She meets my eye, finally.

Abby

I go through the bushes, I'm met by a shirtless Enzo doing up his belt buckle.

"I'm sorry. Colt said you would be done." I mumble stuttering.

Enzo is fit. I wouldn't have guessed it, he hides under the sweaters and old-fashioned coats. His arms are bulging, a six-pack with sharply chiselled muscles ready to burst out of his skin. The setting sun, reflecting off the muscles in a wonderful light.

"Could have called out. What do you want?" He snaps, not bothering he is shirtless.

"I want magical assistance. My head is throbbing."

Casually, he puts on the sweater. "Sit. Let's see what damage you've done."

I do. I can feel my cheeks are red. I blame the fact that I hit my head. Enzo doesn't seem to care or notice. He just waves his hands causing magic to fly. It touches my forehead like a butterfly landing gently. Slowly, pain eases from my head.

"You probably have a concussion." Enzo sighs.

I nod. "Yeah. Can you fix that?"

"I can fix almost anything."

"Is that a yes?"

He sighs like the answer was implied. "Yes, it is done."

"I want to thank you, even if I don't agree with all your methods, I do appreciate you helping Holly." I say.

I'm not going to ask what happened in the forest. Holly was like a hurricane when we found her. Yet, Holly is ecstatic, I just left her to change. She is human. Praising Enzo to the rooftops. I had been worried, she looked terrified when she crashed into us.

Enzo grunts. "Wasn't my idea."

"Yeah, Colt said you weren't too thrilled." I smile seeing if he will return it. He doesn't. "Colt told me the story about how you helped him."

Enzo nods, he doesn't say anything. The nod says he understands, he just doesn't care what I am saying.

"Why were you so eager to help him? Why were you even there?"

I had asked Colt he didn't know the answers. Enzo does. I want the story. Enzo seems to be so secretive but I want to get to know him. He is helping Holly. Enzo doesn't reply or move at all. Enzo's eyes go dark, fading into his own mind.

"Enzo?" I ask.

He blinks, a frown covering his face. "Are you interrogating me now?"

"No. I just want to know."

My shoulders droop to Enzo's defensive stance. Enzo's eyes narrow, my heart beats in the silence. Should I leave? He's fixed my head. I stand. He isn't talking. What is the point?

"Fine," Enzo mutters.

I turn. "What?"

"I'll tell you." Enzo sits on a rock, again. What's wrong with the ground? I settle in the grass, tickling my arms.

"It started three hundred years ago." In shock, my eyes widen, I didn't realise the story would start that long ago. Enzo sees my look, he is ready to stop talking. "Three hundred years ago, seriously?"

"Yes." He states bluntly. "I had a friend Margherita, she was a fairly new vampire and an outstanding drinker. Sadly, she was murdered shortly before her wedding. The husband-to-be killed himself to join her in death."

Enzo's face refuses to let out any emotion. "They left a child behind. A human child. Margherita had before she was turned. It was two-years-old."

"But Colt said he was twenty-one?"

"Colt is as old as he says he is. It's not him. It was Valentina." A soft smile. "I vowed to protect the family line as long as I lived. Margherita deserved to have all her grandchildren safe. I told her I would do it when she died in my arms."

Okay, I was hoping for a more joyful story. Not this.

"I've been following their family line for the last three hundred years. I only interfere when I must."

"You've been his family's guardian angel," I mutter.

I can't believe Enzo did this. Imagine caring for a family for centuries without their knowledge all because of a promise to a late friend.

Enzo grunts. "I tried to save Colt. That's why I was there. I saw him get caught. I just wasn't fast enough. I'll never forgive myself for that. Now he's a vampire and I will protect him for eternity."

I fall silent. Enzo helped Colt because of a vow he made three hundred years ago. I didn't expect this. I thought it would be much simpler. For example, he saw something happen in the area and followed. Found the kids and decided to help out the kindness of his heart.

"What about the other descendants?"

"Dead. Colt is the only one left."

"How did they die?"

"Old age. They were human. I can't save them from life's natural course. The only other one left is Colt's mother, she lost her right to my protection when she disowned Colt. Margherita would be disappointed in her."

I nod in agreement. That is fair.

I fall silent. Imagining, if I had a good friend, dying in my arms. Being left with their child and vowing to protect her entire family line. No matter the cost. That is a hard promise, but Enzo has kept it.

"How did you get the daylight chain?"

Enzo sighs, heavily the bombardment of questions too much for him. "He told you. Fine. Margherita gave it to me as she died."

"Why doesn't Colt know?" I ask, fiddling with grass strands.

"He never asked."

Surely, you would tell someone about their heritage? Especially if it is the sole purpose you helped them. Surely it is important to know? "If someone knew my great grandparents, I would want to know."

"Really?" Enzo glares at me like he knows something I don't.

"Yes," I answer honestly.

"Your very great-grandmother had magic, like me. She tried to murder me about two hundred years ago. I knew the second I heard your last name, you look quite similar to her, but it seems the magic gene died with her."

Is he messing with me? I don't believe Enzo would make a joke. My great grandmother tried to kill Enzo. It would explain his edginess.

"She tried to kill you?" I feel slightly queasy.

If he held something against our grandmother would he hold it against us? Is that why he is so cruel? We shouldn't be held responsible.

Enzo's lips twitch at the sight of me. "You didn't want to know that, huh?"

I open my mouth to say 'yes I did' but that would be lying. Instead, my mouth closes.

"Her name was Maddie Dean." Enzo clamps his hands together. "She tried to seduce me once, then she just went for it after I couldn't be charmed. Let's just say, I was the one digging a grave that night."

"You..you... killed her?" I exclaim in surprise. How many people has Enzo killed? He says it casually, which makes it worse.

"I had to. I prefer my life over someone else's especially if they are trying to kill me."

Colt appears out of the bushes, smiling. "Come on, it's getting dark."

CHAPTER FIVE

Silven

It's time for my escape. Today is the day I get to spread my wings. I will make that scum of a Queen regret everything she has done. Alex is a terrible Queen, she is not fit to rule Hell. Firstly, she is never here, she chooses to meddle with humans. Humans, disgusting creatures. Her power is incredible but no match for Lucifer. Not at his full strength. I will revive him to his full health, no matter the cost. The vexing human I sent on the mission has till dusk to find me a vessel for when I break loose. I start digging a hole in the dry dead earth. The hole large enough to trip even the swiftest demon. Giving time for my escape. I simply need to reach one of the five portals out of Hell. Then I'll transport to my vessel. I'll gather my ingredients and sacrifices to revive Lucifer. Ten times stronger. Ten times more deadly. Together, we'll rule the whole Hell plain.

On-time, the door opens. I jump away from the hole. The shadows in the cell make it unnoticeable. Arms wrap around me, manhandling me out the cage. Only today, he'll be stuck in the cage, not me.

Hell's Daughter

Abby

Back at school, I yawn aloud at the back of my class, struggling to stay awake. I think about last night. We stayed up together until four am. Talking around a bonfire, Holly was chirpy. The first transformation has helped her a lot. Enzo even smiled a few times and laughed once. He is no less secretive. He received a text. He wouldn't share who from but probably something important. Colt was happy, showing off his skills again. Holly and Colt got in a play fight. I played referee. Colt won all three times but Holly was surprisingly good for someone with no training. The new werewolf genes I suppose.

"Abby Dean!" I jump in my seat, almost falling off the edge. "Pay attention!" My teacher snaps, Enzo talks in a very similar tone.

I smile slightly, Colt waves from his desk. I wave back. "You okay?" He mouths. I nod.

Finally, the teacher stops talking and leaves us to do work while he plays games on his phone under his desk.

"Hi." I spin like a skittish cat in my seat.

It is Callum. The boy I sit next to in food tech. We don't usually talk unless we are asking each other to pass equipment.

The teacher looks up. "Start cooking. The recipe is on the board for the individuals who don't listen." A glare in my direction. He has a point.

I sigh, picking up the flour.

"I heard what you did at the party." Callum smiles, weighing out sugar. "Very brave."

"Thanks." I shrug.

"Did it bite you?"

"No."

Callum nods, taking the flour when I finish. "It's very impressive. I was wondering if you would like to go to the park later with my mates. They'll be alcohol and no wolves."

"Oh, I can't."

"You are turning down a party?" Callum laughs. "What can't you possibly miss?"

"It's Holly, I can't leave her."

"Bring her, and your friends." Callum offers.

"We already have something planned, sorry."

"Another time?" Callum suggests.

"Sure."

Callum proceeds to drone on for the rest of the lesson, suddenly very talkative. He discusses the party, the wolf, taking an interest in my life. Like it matters to him. He asks what is so important I'd miss the party, and where I am going. I understand, I never miss a party. I gave him quick answers trying to turn the conversation back to him. In the end, while turning on my oven, I just nod phasing out to think about what we might do tonight. I'm not in the mood to talk. Enzo isn't teaching today but Holly doesn't mind. Even if he did chase her through the woods. Because his methods are efficient. I wish I could do more, I can't. I'll be there for emotional support. Today she will be learning to control her emotions to prevent unnecessary transformations. Enzo wants someone with her at all times but we refused to bunk because of his worrying. Holly isn't the type to get mad often. Colt and I both stay in food technology without a worry. Holly is generally a laid-back person. But that wasn't good enough, Enzo couldn't pass for a student, he looks at least early to mid-twenties. Instead, he is a substitute teacher today, currently for Holly's class. Somehow, he was able to set it up. I feel bad for those students, I sort of wish I could be there. Enzo doesn't seem to like the type of person who would be good at teaching a bunch of teens. Callum stands, I snap into reality. Colt works in the station opposite us.

"Look after my pie? The teacher wants me." Callum points to the door.

"Sure." I smile. Thank god he is going.

Hell's Daughter

Enzo

The children run around like lost rabbits in a forest. They scatter around the room in huddles, books and paper fly. My fingers itch, the temptation to glue them all to their seats and lock up their mouths is too much. Sadly, I believe they would notice my hands or realise I would be the only one able to move.

"Sit down." I bark. "I don't give a shit what you are trying to do. Sit down now!"

Holly chuckles from the front as I try to control the class. I've taught before. Last time it wasn't humans. For this very reason. They slowly sit down. Two whole minutes are taken to sit their asses on a damn seat. Now the lesson, it would be good if I knew anything about babies. I mean the cover work looks terrible. Who teaches a course on social care? Learning how to not kill a baby is a course? How stupid do they have to be to kill a baby? I sit at my desk, secretly searching up what to do on my phone under the desk. They don't notice while they talk. I have a double lesson with these creatures. A boy walks in ten minutes late to the class.

"Who are you?" I call as he goes for an empty seat.

"Callum, sorry. I got held up."

I shrug, I don't care where he has been. I wave for him to sit, he places himself next to Holly. My phone loads a list of the curriculum for the course. Good.

Ten minutes later, I have a quiz on the screen which they complete quietly enough. The slides change automatically. My phone buzzes. A text from Alex, the Queen of Hell. Alex had needed me for some work a few years back, we exchanged numbers in cases she needed my services again. Only she also uses it whenever she wants to talk. God knows why. She has plenty of people to talk to. I smile, reading the message, it's a complaint about her brother's son, Ricky. A toddler. I met him once. He's sweet, I guess. I mean he's a baby it's hard to have an opinion. Flint has another child who is ten but I've never met him. Alex doesn't take care of him as often. I ask her what to do with the class after the quiz. She has to know what to do, or I have no hope. This is a double lesson. Callum, the boy who was late in, is getting all the answers wrong. Holly is laughing with him. My phone rings.

I read the message. 'It's baby caring isn't it? Summon a dozen babies and make them care for them. Duh.' I laugh. I mean it's an idea… I can't…

Another bleep. 'You can have Ricky. Please.' That gets an eye roll.

The quiz on the board reaches the last two questions. There is an hour and ten minutes of the lesson left. Shit. I like Alex's jokes but I really need a suggestion. Or a dozen babies will go missing for an hour. Under the desk, I flick my fingers. A dozen sheets of paper with information on how to teach human children. A chocolate bar as well.

"Add up your points. Highest tally gets a chocolate bar." I wave it.

Excitedly, they grab their paper to count with new enthusiasm. I didn't need to be taught that. I read the book, fake babies. I could give them fake babies. Then what?

"I got twenty!" A voice hollers.

Shoot. They've counted. I give out the chocolate bar to the winner. A girl sitting alone in the back corner who got thirty.

"Hey!" Holly's distinctive voice is heard over the others. I spin, her eyes are a fading yellow colour. I glare, how can she not tell?

"He pinched me." She holds her arm, which holds a red mark.

I sigh, is that it? He pinched her arm. I've been stabbed and I made less of a fuss.

"Callum, move over there," I order.

He moves, wordlessly. I hope no-one has noticed her eyes.

"Your eyes are glowing." I hiss.

Hell's Daughter

"He pinched me," Holly growls back.

"Calm down. Or people will see." I glare.

Rage flares in her eyes, but she takes a deep breath. The yellow tint fades. I sigh, the other two swore that Holly would be alright. They were wrong and I was right, that is no surprise.

At that moment, Alex waltzes into the classroom.

"What the hell?" I mutter.

Alex sways in, Ricky on her hip. A tubby baby with a balled-up fist. The baby is crying madly.

"I'm done." Alex holds the baby at arms' length. All the students stare. I understand why when Alex walks in she literally glows. Caramel skin, glowing from spending so much time in Hell.

"Who wants to hold a baby?" Alex announces.

The class clamours, snapping out their trance. They nod eagerly like a puppy given a tennis ball. Alex dumps the baby in the first person's lap who was meant to be sitting next to Callum but he's gone. The baby stops balling. I shrug. An uproar of 'awww' and 'let me hold him' erupts from the class.

"Seems like I only need one baby." I raise my eyebrow at the students. "Will Ricky be okay?"

"Yes. They are only humans." Alex shrugs, jumping on my desk.

"Why are you here?" I ask.

"Because I want to. If you do remember I am the Queen of Hell. I can do what I please."

"I didn't forget." I lean back in the chair, my back clicks. The students stress me out. If I try to prevent a transformation some of my joints can go stiff.

"Magic me a chocolate bar, caramel please," Alex demands.

I do as she asks. The children aren't looking anyway. They are too busy with the baby. Other than Holly who makes her way over to us.

"Who is this?" Holly stares at Alex in awe.

Alex grows excited. "Is this your girlfriend? A little young for you, don't you think? And a werewolf. New and confused I can tell." Alex examines.

"I'm a lesbian." Holly corrects her.

Alex winks. "Even better."

Holly goes bright red at the meaningless flirting. "I have a girlfriend."

Alex nods, biting into the chocolate. "Okay, I'll steer clear."

Holly watches Alex. She can't help it. Alex is a magnet, everything is drawn to her. A perk of being the most powerful being in the universe.

"Is that your baby?" Holly waves to Ricky.

Alex laughs. "No, my brother's. I do not have a baby! Hell no."

"Who are you?"

I glance at Alex and shake my head. She pauses, stopping the announcement of her royalty. "I'm Alex, a friend of Enzo's. A witch."

Holly grins. "Really? Cool!"

Silently, I thank her. She smiles slyly my way. Alex has a keen eye for all supernaturals, she understands Holly isn't ready to know.

"Don't you have a lesson to get back to?" Alex shoos her away.

Holly nods, scampering away.

"Who is she? What are you doing here?" Alex raises a questioning eyebrow. "Why are you teaching humans?" Her nose shrivels. "I don't think it is your area of expertise."

"Don't ask." I sigh rubbing my forehead.

Alex bites in the chocolate laughing. "I get it. I won't ask."

I swing back in my chair. "You must be really bored to come see me."

Alex's eyes roll heavier than mine do. I magic up a coffee. Alex scoops it up before I can get my hands on it. She chugs the hot liquid. Instantly, it comes spewing out her mouth. Wheezing, she coughs up the coffee. The desk and floor, soaking in the drink. I laugh. I knew she would take it.

"What is that?" Alex whips her mouth.

"Remember when we went to France?" I give her a hint.

"There were snails in there!" The mug aims for my head. I block it, the mug disappearing with a dismissive wave.

I chuckle. I loved France, the city lights and the music are beautiful. Alex and I spent a week there four years ago. We went to the top of the Eiffel Tower, leaning off the very tip. We took a hot air balloon around the city or we tried. Half an hour in we found our way into a ditch. We went to some amazing restaurants. That is where Alex forced me to try snails, promising that they were delicious. I did, they were disgusting and I swore revenge. Alex didn't touch them, I should have known.

"I think I swallowed one." Alex coughs. "It is so slimy. At least the ones you ate were cooked, asshole. I'm going to get you back for this."

I grin. "You deserve it."

Abby

Holly texts me, we are meeting in her classroom so we can go off to the forest for her training. It is so she can avoid Selena. Holly has been texting Selena non-stop but can't face her yet. Not till she is convinced she has it under control. Otherwise, she might turn while kissing Selena. Any strong emotions can set it off. She would never want to hurt Selena. Thankfully, the lesson finally ends and we leave to meet them.

Walking in with Colt, my eyes immediately go to the woman sitting on the teacher's desk. I can't help it. Her hair bobs as she laughs. She is beautiful. She looks flawless, her nose arcs just enough, her smile reveals perfect teeth. There is something that calls out 'look at me' and she knows it. It's like everything is drawn to her, even the light. She has an amazing figure which she shows off gracefully. I snap out of it, approaching the desk. Behind her, I see who is making her laugh. Enzo, with a half-smile on his face. I rub my eyes, am I dreaming? Nope. They are sitting there together.

"Enzo do you have a girlfriend?" I grin in approval. They look good together.

"No." He snorts.

"He wishes." The girl swings her legs over to face us, she is wearing tight leather trousers, green eyes sparkling.

Holly holds a baby tightly.

"Who is this?" I swoon, rushing to the baby, it grabs my finger.

A sigh. "Ricky keeps stealing my thunder." The woman scoops up the baby. "My name is Alex."

I nod, watching Ricky giggle sweetly. "He's adorable."

"I'll let my brother and his wife know."

"Oh…" He's not hers. I coo at the baby, he bubbles happily.

"I should go," Alex announces. "Enzo portal me."

"Of course."

My eyes widen. Enzo is always ordering us around. Yet, Alex can just tell him what to do and he does it without complaining. No, 'I'm doing this because I have to' look. I'm sure if I tried to make Enzo do something, he would yell my ear off. They walk to the doorway. Alex whispers something in Enzo's ear. He chuckles, checking outside the door for any witnesses. A portal forms. Alex hugs him, Enzo doesn't pull back. He hugs her back. What is this? Alex laughs at something Enzo murmurs. He's made someone laugh. Alex kisses his cheek, clutching Ricky. Enzo, who I thought would never be a baby person, sends off magic sparks to make the baby smile. They disappear before my eyes as they go through the portal. My jaw is on the floor. Quickly, I collect myself before he turns around.

"What happened to Enzo?"

Enzo scowls at me. "What?"

I chuckle. "Okay. He's back."

"Why couldn't she make her own portal, she is a witch." Holly interrupts.

Colt bursts into a fit of laughter. "That's not a witch." Colt shakes his head.

"Who is she then?" Holly demands.

"She is Alex, Queen of Hell." The most powerful demon alive." Enzo answers. "She could very easily make her own portal. She just likes to use me."

My eyes widen, in the book, Alex and her family have their own section. I read she took down Lucifer a few years back. Lucifer, exists. I just met his daughter. The most powerful person alive. Well, demon. According to the book, she can kill anyone with a snap of her fingers. How did I not work it out when she told us her name?

"Abby. Abby." Enzo snaps his fingers in my face. I jump in response.

"I don't get it. Before you acted like you barely knew her."

"Know her? They are practically dating." Colt chuckles.

Enzo rolls his eyes dismissively. Another wave of hands and a new portal appears.

"Come on. We need to go." Enzo urges us along.

Colt wraps a hand around my shoulder. "Let's go."

We appear in the forest. The dark tree bark is the same as yesterday, but we seem to be in a different spot. Colt shucks his jacket, Enzo leans against a tree, his phone out. Completely ignoring us. I sigh.

"What are we doing?" Holly asks.

"Practising our fighting skills while also controlling yourself."

Holly nods, ditching the baggy sweater.

"Okay, tell me when to begin." Holly raises her fist awkwardly. My sister is good and spent most of her childhood inside reading. She never gets in arguments and has never been in a fight. Last night was fun, but this is an actual fight.

"On three." Colt smiles my way. "Want to countdown?"

I get to play referee again.

"Okay. The first one to get the other to the ground wins. No powers." Colt sets the ground rules.

Holy looks unprepared. "Three." I move to the sideline. "Two." As the word leaves my mouth, Colt sends a punch for Holly's nose. Sprawling, she lands on the ground, nose bleeding over her lip. I gasp. "Holly!"

"That's cheating!" Holly spits.

One of Holly's pet peeves, cheaters. Holly can chew my ear off moaning about cheaters. She never calls them out, she hates arguments. She hates how they get away with it. In her eyes a yellow tint, nails growing.

"I said no powers." Colt jeers. "Who is cheating now? Control it." He calls.

Holly takes a few deep breaths, the claws retract. Jumping, her fist connects with his jaw, sending him sailing Enzo, Enzo side steps without looking up. Colt smacks into the tree.

"Yes, Holly!" I cheer, clapping.

She smiles, wolf teeth retracting.

"Look out!" I holler.

Colt kicks her in the stomach, using super-speed to swoop down and take her out by the legs.

"Stop cheating!" Holly howls, sounding much like a bark.

Holly swings a punch, Colt dodges using speed. I can't see him move. Just popping up, as if he portalled between spots. Holly screams in outrage.

"Control it! Reel it in." Colt says softly.

A bone cracks, Holly kicks him in the shin forcing him to buckle. Colt bounces back to his feet.

"Yes, Holly!" I cheer. "Kick his ass."

"Hey. Don't I get a motivational cheer too?" Colt smiles.

"No! I want you to lose."

Colt flips himself over Holly's shoulder, getting her square in the back all while giving me the middle finger. I give it back. In the brief moment of distraction, Holly sends a kick at his head. Suddenly, a blue force field sends Holly flying backward. Enzo is off his phone, the glow fades from his hands.

"Hey!" Holly snaps.

"You can't interfere with the game," I call out.

"No rule against me using magic." Enzo shrugs.

Holly howls, lips twitching. They are breaking the rules to get on her nerves and it is working.

"Control it," Colt tells her gently.

Taking deep breaths, her back hunches. If they are fighting as a team, we can too. I pounce on Colt's back. "Holly!" Holly reacts, getting him in the face, blood splattering. I drop onto the ground, Colt shaking me off. Holly goes to make a move. An arrow whistles, thwacking a tree behind us. Blood trickles down Holly's ear.

"Enzo!" I hiss, weapons are too far. "What the hell!"

He stares in the direction of the arrow. "It wasn't me."

Another arrow flies. "Get down!" Enzo yells in urgency, tackling me to the ground.

An arrow whizzes by where my head had been. That would have killed me. Another arrow flies through the air. My heart starts to hammer.

CHAPTER SIX

Silven

I stumble at the shove from my guard as we make our way back to my cell after yet another day of torture. Alex uses me as a reminder of what would happen if they betray her. Demons are good at torturing but don't always take it well. Not for long. This is my chance. The cell door opens. Swinging, the guard goes to slam the door. Swiftly I spin, snatching the chain around his neck. It snaps the key entering my palm. Cackling, I grasp it. Step one complete. Ordinary demons really aren't that smart.

"Hey!" The demon snarls.

Skidding, I make a break for it. The guard lunges, stepping into the pothole. I dodge, escaping from my rotten cell. In a second, I'm outside the cell locking the door. A shiver of satisfaction, I did it. I bolt. The screeching noise of the alarm begins. I have to get to Earth before it's too late. My rags drag along the floor while I charge for the portal. I pass rows of empty cells. There is no-one else down here except Lucifer. I don't dare look at him, I will be back for him. I keep running. He's been cast to Hell and cannot escape. I need to go to Earth to break the

Hell's Daughter

spell holding him here. Twenty demons, on their unique set of limbs, block my exit. Some slow, some fast but all deadly. Struggling, I try to undo my shackles without stopping. They charge. The keys jingle in my hands as I shove them in the lock. Snapping them free, I cackle. Finally, my wrists are loose. My muddy black hair swishing in my face as I raise the wind. The tornado rattles torches, the bars of the cells bend inward. The hurricane blasts the soldiers in every direction. Howling, they sail into walls with graceful smacks. I missed the power to control the movement of air. I missed power in general, I grew hungrier for it each day. The hurricane is so graceful swarming above everyone else. Running for the gate, my hooves clip on the hellstone. The noise music to my ears. Finally, I am able to roam free. The portal is left from here. Behind me, the soldiers have recovered charging in their pathetic efforts to stop me. My hands swirl the wind, knocking over a demon tower behind me. My power is too great for them to handle. I laugh, not looking back. The portal awaits, three storeys high and glowing in the shape of an oval. The edges begin to fold in, the red magic replacing the black shutters.

The circle shrinks before my eyes, I didn't prepare for this. I don't hear the tower hit the ground, I know I blew it over. I feel arms grab me, I howl. I can't lose this opportunity. There won't be another. The portal is half a metre away. My fingers brush it, I can make it. My withering heart pumps, I gather all my strength sending a wave through the crowd howling. The guards spew over the dirty plain. Taking the moment of freedom, I tumble through the portal. The broken sound of Hell echoing behind me. My minion better have my human ready for me to transfer into.

Abby

My heart pounds. Mud blinds me as I army crawl in a bush. Enzo blasts magic at the attacker. Or tries to. The darkness hides their position. We could die. The thought makes my head spin and my stomach churn. In the thick bushes I cling to Holly.

"Here." Colt presses a knife in my hand. "If you need it."

A knife sits in my palm. It isn't a kitchen knife. It's a blade to kill. The blade curves at the end for more damage, I suppose. A minute ago, we were teenagers hanging out. Now we might die. An arrow flies over my head. I can hear the gentle ping of a bow. The attacker is getting closer. I grip the knife harder with a sweaty palm.

"Stay here," Colt whispers urgently.

I clutch Holly who is shaking. Colt disappears out of sight. What is going on? Colt and Enzo are nowhere to be seen.

I hear the trees rustle. The same noise when Colt and I ran through the forest. I remember the forest blurring into an array of magnificent greens and browns. I couldn't breathe, the air racing away before I could grasp it. My eyes watering due to the speed. I have never felt so free and happy. The giddy feeling causing me to giggle. I gripped Colt so hard to stop myself from falling, desperate to make it last as long as possible, my hair blowing in my face. I wanted to remain in that moment forever. I take a deep breath, I can't be a wimp now.

"Will you be okay?" I ask Holly.

She nods, but her non-stop shaking suggests otherwise. A thump. I look up over the bush. Colt is smashing a head into a tree, looking very heroic doing it. I see who the boy is. Callum from my class. Enzo sends a bolt of magic at Callum. His body spasms flopping to the ground. I look over, Callum doesn't move.

"Holly. He's down." I hope not dead.

"Really?"

"Yes."

She stops shivering. Looking over, she sighs in relief. Enzo lifts a powerful hand. "Don't kill him!"

Everyone turns to glance at me as I say it. I don't realise, but I mean it.

"Why ever not?" Enzo scrunches up his nose.

"He's not going anywhere Enzo. Don't kill him." Colt answers, supporting my decision.

"Fine," Enzo grumbles, lowering his hands.

"What a stupid kid." Colt bends down next to the unconscious body. "What made him think he would win?"

"Why would he attack at all?" Holly asks, eyes wide.

Colt's face goes grim, drawing his lips into a fine line.

"Chances are that he hates supernaturals." Enzo goes right for the punch.

Holly sits down by his body, slowing watching his face as if she expects his eyes to open. I stand behind them. Holly hates the idea of being a werewolf and this doesn't make it any better.

"He was going to kill us?" Holly's face is drawn.

"Yes." Colt answers.

"For what we are." Holly wants confirmation.

"Get used to it." Enzo shrugs.

"The bastard!" Holly spits, anger in her eyes with a hint of a yellow glow.

Thank god, I thought she would react worse than that. He is a bastard. A smile plays on Enzo's lips to her answer.

Suddenly, Callum jumps to his feet. His hands wrap around Holly's throat. A silver blade going for her neck. I reach out but I'm too late. I can't grab her, he's backed up too far. My heart pounds worse than ever.

Callum spins to face Colt and Enzo. "Move and I kill her."

Enzo scowls, fingers pausing while Colt's teeth glisten.

"Don't move." He threatens.

My brain swarms with suggestions trying to find a reasonable way out of this. The knife moves closer to her neck, and all logic I hold disappears. Next thing I know I'm on Callum's back raising the knife Colt had given me. Jabbing it into his arm forcing him to release his grip on the knife, Holly takes the opportunity to escape his grasp.

I pull out the knife, snarling. "Don't you dare hurt my sister!"

I go to stab again, this time into his back. Plunging it in, Callum swings his arm and I soar across the clearing. My body shudders as I sail into a tree. My back snaps on the tree trunk. I howl out in agony. The knife goes for my heart. In a daze, I stretch out a hand to stop it. My back throbbing wildly.

My hand slips, allowing the knife to pass through, ripping open my skin. Entering my chest, I gasp the cold silver striking pain through my body. Tears pour down my cheeks, my lung aches as the knife passes through. The stinging pain pulsing in my chest, my head ringing. Colt rushes forward, not soon enough. The knife connects again, to the left of my chest. I scream feeling my flesh rip open. I wheeze, blood spilling out of my body like a fountain. My eyes widen. There is so much. I clutch my wounds, struggling to breathe. My eyesight begins to fade.

Callum fights with Colt on the ground. They wrestle in a flurry. I watch Enzo send out streaks of colourful magic striking Callum and he stops moving.

"No!" Holly screams, her brown hair falls in my face.

I try to smile but I can't... I can't there are shooting pains all over my body. I can't straighten my back or move at all. The world slips sideways definitely not the way it's meant to. I can't move, it is too painful. My back feels like it's on fire. I fight my eyes while they flutter. My chest is numb, the red warm liquid sticking to my hands that sit on my chest.

"No! No! No! He got her chest." Holly sobs. "Heal her!"

"I'm on it." Enzo hisses batting her out the way.

My eyes droop softly. The panic subsides to a giddy happiness. The pain subsiding, a small joyful moment. My hormones spiking. At least I have Holly and Colt. I'm possibly happy for Enzo too. Swaying, my eyes begin to shut. My head droops, a gaping hole in my chest oozing fresh blood.

"Don't sleep." Holly orders. "Stay awake!"

I try to listen but it is impossible as I drift off into nothingness.

Enzo

I barely have time to raise my hands and Colt is bashing in Callum's head, splitting his skull. I can applaud him later.

Callum's eyes flicker. "Kill me, I have served my purpose."

I blast a pulse of magic instantly taking down the bastard. The magic sending a wave through his body, knocking him out. The threat is gone, I bend over Abby to examine her.

"Heal her!" Holly begs.

"I'm on it!" I snap shoving her out my way.

Abby is no longer bright and bubbly but fragile and weak. The knife wound in her left lung and heart is a fatal injury for a human. I sigh, I am not afraid she will die. I know she'll live. Death isn't even a possibility I will consider. I won't let it happen. My hands surge magic into the wound healing her slowly. Abby's eyes close, her head couldn't stay up any longer. I can hear her steady heartbeat. Holly screams for Abby to wake up in my ear and starts shaking. I flick a spark in her direction. She darts backwards and her mouth zips up. I don't want a distraction.

The blade is already out which means nothing is blocking the blood flow outwards. Blood pours out over all our clothes and stains the grass. Colt is shedding his shirt in a second, holding it upon the fatal wound in the heart. The magic starts its job. The beating is getting slower, I know Colt can hear it. I work faster, repairing each cell one at a time. I work at the appropriate speed, it isn't a hard procedure, but it must be done well. I can fix small cuts in seconds. This wound has hit her heart, if it is not done properly, I could kill her. Abby's heartbeat is faint. There is a small amount of internal bleeding, I deal with that first. It takes years to master healing the body. I had to learn to do this like a doctor learns to do surgery. Using the wrong magic could kill her. I've had plenty of experience on my own wounds. Her back is leaking blood everywhere. Colt's shirt is soaking. Steadily, I begin to fix the heart wound, the threads of pulling the flesh back together, the blood vessel interlinking. The scar tissue on her chest closing up but I can no longer hear her heart pumping. The second wound in her ribs pools blood.

"Enzo!" Colt panics.

"Leave. I will fix her. I need ten minutes." I meant it when I said I wouldn't let her die.

Colt looks torn between staying or going.

"Ten minutes, I promise."

Listening, Colt picks up Holly and leaves the clearing begrudgingly. Holly struggles against him, but the magic keeps her silent. I check Abby's pulse, she is dead. I have two options, fix the second wound, fix her back, give her CPR and pray or use a foolproof alternative. Digging in my pocket, I pull out a small glass bottle. It is no bigger than my thumb but it is enough. Popping open the lid, the liquid glimmers. Feeding it through Abby's dead lips, I wait till the bottle empties. It's done. She'll wake up in a few seconds.

I won't admit it out loud but I admire her. She jumped in the way of her sister when we couldn't. It was reckless no doubt, it killed her. The red liquid stains her lips, trickling down the corner of her mouth. My Hellhound ears hear her heartbeat start again, steady and constant. Under the torn shirt, the scars disappear. The breaths deep, pulling oxygen back to her lungs. All her wounds healed. Quietly she moans in her sleep. I should take back what I said, with what I gave her she should be in better shape than me. My eyes catch rustling leaves, I spin. The clearing is empty. Abby gasps, I look back to her. Abby's eyes open wide, a grin on her face. I sigh in relief, finally.

Silven

Rising up from Hell, I find myself in a forest in a ring of burnt grass. Freedom. Easing forward, my hooves sink in the grass. I'm on Earth, after all this time. Joy fills my body, I did it. I can smell the sweetness of dew, the Earth is too pure. That will change soon enough. Lucifer and I can destroy Earth. My nose perks up at the smell of a freshly dead body. I smirk, death is so perfect.

Easing forward, my disciple has done well. My hooves ache to run on the crisp grass, I restrain the urge to run. The cramped cell was too small to move more than a few steps. I stretch out my legs. Waltzing through the trees, I see a young male, his blood splattering on the gracious oak wood, the crimson fluid has a very sweet smell. Looking closer, I can see the bone in his skull crushed. I smile faintly. Turning, the child chosen for my possession lies on the ground. Enzo, the son of a bitch is there. If only I could kill him now. But I can't. Back on Earth, my powers are weak. My presence is temporary until I enter a human body. Not many demons can stay on Earth without a body unless they have Alex's approval. I am merely a phantom at this point. I slip over to them. Enzo leans over the body, the bastard. A vial lays on the ground, probably a potion. The girl is pretty, I can certainly charm a few girls and boys with her. Enzo's head spins in my direction when I reach a few steps away. He can't see me, but I don't want to risk that he can sense me.

I touch the girl, my entire body jolts. My limbs convulse, as my presence fades away. I enter the girl, her body mine to control. I will use her to make sacrifices to save my king. I feel the human body envelop me. I will have full control. I did it. I avoided execution and I can rescue Lucifer. I laugh. Enzo will not know what hit him.

CHAPTER SEVEN

Abby

I gasp my eyes wide. Enzo leans over my body, Colt and Holly are nowhere to be seen. I'm alive. I clutch my chest, there are no wounds. Not even a scar. I sigh in relief, hugging myself tight. That was close. I am alive. My shirt is torn open, another shirt on my stomach. I remove the bloody shirt from my stomach. My eyes widen, it is like it never happened. The wounds are completely gone, there aren't even scars. My back, I can straighten it. My arm doesn't hurt anymore. I don't feel any pain. A significant amount of blood drenches my clothes.

"Finally." Enzo rolls his eyes.

"How long was I out for?" I ask. It's still dark, I can't have been out longer than an hour.

"Three minutes."

I almost died, and three minutes is too long to be unconscious for? I take a deep breath, I can't be mad. He is the one who saved me.

"Thanks."

Enzo shrugs, waving his hand, I appear in new clothes. To my surprise, they are my style. A pair of black skinny jeans with a crop white shirt with the word 'live' across the chest in black lettering with a black denim jacket over it.

I chuckle. "Is this a souvenir or a reminder?"

I point to the shirt. Enzo does have a sense of humour.

"Both." Enzo answers.

My jeans are folded up the cuffs, I am wearing high heel black boots all laced up. They are very pretty. Moving my foot, I hear a small crunch, I look under my foot and there is a small cracked glass tube. Red stains the lip of the bottle.

"What is this?" I pick it up.

"Nothing." Enzo snatches it back abruptly.

"Is it blood? Enzo? What is it?" The tube is empty, I'm certain he used the content on me.

"Magic healing was taking too long and Colt and Holly were panicking so I chose the fastest route."

Blood, the fastest route? That is very vague. I can taste blood in my mouth, I touch my lip. Red liquid stains my fingers.

"I'm not a vampire, am I?" I ask, praying it isn't true even if all the signs point that way.

"What? No." Enzo rolls his eyes as if the question were ridiculous. "I suppose I should explain."

"You think?" I point to the bottle. "Did I drink this?"

"Alex, her blood can bring back the dead, heal people as if it never happened," Enzo answers casually. "When you died, I used it."

"I died?" I touch my chest gently. My heart pounds, I died. "I came back to life?"

"Yes. As a human. Not a vampire."

I died. That doesn't seem real but I am alive now and that is what matters I suppose. Thank god. I am human and alive. I didn't even consider the fact I could die. I'm too young to die.

Enzo snaps his fingers to get my attention. "Hey!"

Hell's Daughter

"I read the book, it never said that Alex could bring people back to life."

"No, it doesn't. Alex's capability is a secret. Tell anyone, I'll kill you. Better yet, she probably will."

"Seriously?" He saved my life and is threatening to take it in a matter of minutes.

A shrug. "Some are smart enough that they can work it out. Alex is half-angel half-demon. Angels can heal humans from anything with a tiny dose of their blood. Alex inherited that power too."

"Are there more half angels?"

"No. They are a pure breed, excluding Alex."

I hug my knees, thankful I am here. Angels are higher beings. They have no ruler and decide who lives and who dies only the purest of people can become one after death. Demons, on the other hand, are evil and kill for fun. They are known to be troublemakers. Alex is half and half.

"Thanks to her blood you are alive. You can't tell Colt or Holly, let them believe my magic saved you."

I nod. "Okay."

I can imagine Holly wouldn't be able to handle the information she is still getting used to it all. I will assume Enzo has a good reason for not telling Colt and I will respect that.

"Wait, how come you know, if it's a secret?"

"The secret isn't held as well as she'd like. The reason she doesn't spread it is obvious. People will do a lot when they are desperate. No-one can kill her, but there are other things people can do. I know because we are friends."

I gasp. "You admit you have friends?"

Enzo sighs. "I thought you'd have been able to decipher that from her saving my ass with that class."

I chuckle, I feel amazing. I haven't felt this good in ages. "More important question: why do you have her blood?"

"It was a gift."

I frown, that is highly vague. Enzo is secretive but for the Queen of Hell to gift Enzo something so powerful, there must be a reason. He is hiding something.

"How did you become friends with the Queen of Hell?" Bingo, he flinches.

"I helped her." He admits. "I trapped Lucifer in Hell. She needed a binder, a warlock from both Hell and Earth. I'm part Hellhound which is from Hell and Warlocks who are from Earth. I control the bond that keeps him there. That is how we met."

How do I respond to that? Enzo holds Lucifer in Hell. I can barely believe that Satan exists. Or he has children. There is Hell and Heaven. It is incredible.

"She thought she would have to force me or bribe me to help her." Enzo relaxes on the tree. "I did it willingly, I liked her the second she walked through the door. I knew she would do better than Lucifer."

"She must like you too if she keeps coming back."

A smile. "We did become friends. No-one else knows what I've told you."

"Why not tell other people?"

Enzo is very secretive about everything, even to the people he's close to. Colt doesn't seem to mind. I want to know, it seems important to know. Especially if you spend time with someone. It is part of being friends, Enzo doesn't get it.

"Word can spread, if someone can smell a secret, they'll do anything to find out. I don't tell Colt so he can't be forced to say what he doesn't know."

I guess that justification makes sense. He does it because he cares, but what does that say about his feelings towards me? I smile to myself.

"Why did she give you her blood?"

"It was a gift to say thank you."

"How many vials?"

"Ten."

Hell's Daughter

Ten. Ten chances to save a life. Ten chances to bring back a life. That's all.

"I only use it in desperate situations," Enzo explains.

"How many have you used?" I ask out of curiosity.

"One in the last 10 years." He waves the small bottle he holds.

I swear my heart misses a beat. He has only used one. One for me. I wouldn't be here if he hadn't used it to save my life. He has ten opportunities to save a life and he uses one on me.

"Thanks." I smile. "I haven't said that yet, have I?"

"No. I was waiting for that."

"How many would you have used in the last five hundred years if you could?"

"One hundred and twenty-one." He answers in an instant taking no time to calculate.

Holy shit. One hundred twenty-one people that Enzo has cared about have died. In only five hundred years. The pain he must feel. How did they all die? If I lost Holly I would be crushed. I don't think I could ever be the same again. The emotional pain would be overwhelming.

"What?" Enzo scowls.

I shake my head, I must have given him a look. His light mood is gone and his defences are back up. "Sorry. I-I can't imagine losing that many people."

"Of course not." Enzo sighs. "You are human."

"You had to watch your family grow old and die." I murmur.

I hadn't thought about it. I can call my parents whenever I want to. I know Colt's parents are alive, even if they are assholes. I hadn't thought about Enzo's.

"Didn't you read about Warlocks and Hellhounds?" Enzo snaps.

I did. I think back to the book. Warlocks don't die. Hellhounds live for about two hundred to six hundred years. They should still be here. Where are they?

"They were murdered. I tried to save them but I couldn't." Regret and hurt enter Enzo's voice.

They are dead. I understand why Enzo is so cold and brutal. His family is dead, everyone he cares about is dead. That would destroy anyone with a heart. I wouldn't want to feel anymore. I would live in constant worry that I would lose anyone I got close to.

"Stop looking at me like that." Enzo rises to his feet.

"Sorry. I guess I finally realise why you are closed off. I understand now."

"You thought I was always cold?" A heavy shake of his head.

Before I can snap back a response, Holly and Colt emerge.

"Abby!" Holly runs in my arms. I embrace her, grinning from ear to ear. I squeeze her tightly, words couldn't say how happy I am to see her.

Enzo

I tell Abby everything. Shock constantly over her face. Colt knows as much, just told over a longer time. Well, most of it. I would tell Colt more, but he is under threat. It is no secret that I took Colt in. If someone wanted information about me, they would go to him. It is safer for him if he doesn't know. Abby on the other hand, no-one will suspect I will tell her. I doubt we will even be communicating in a few months. I wouldn't tell her anything but it is the way Abby will trust me. That is what Colt needs. Abby is in shock, she expresses that she understands why I am brutal and cold-hearted. I want to laugh, she can't understand. That's why I like Colt, he doesn't pretend to understand. To understand you must go through it. The imagination is much less brutal than the reality.

Hell's Daughter

I remember when I was kinder and more outgoing. I'd go to many parties. I wore a long tail navy suit and a top hat with a cloak. I looked very dapper. My hair was free of hair gel, I didn't enjoy it when that was popular. My hair was shoulder length with a few curls going wild. The women passed in their beautiful dresses and danced, like an array of flowers swaying in a field. They giggled tipsily at my jokes. They flirted back equally as much. I didn't have much competition, I was considered quite good-looking back then, 'a proper bachelor' it was said. It was all fun and games. I can recall the crystal hearts in the chandelier sending the candlelight throughout the entire grand ballroom. The gentle beat of the piano playing classical music. The singer, her voice was breathtaking I could have sworn she was an angel. Ashley was her name. She was who I ended up with that night. Smart, beautiful, charming Ashley. I remember her soft curly hair, her dark silky bronze skin, her eyes. They were a beautiful gentle brown in the darkness. She was the kindest person I had ever met. Ashley died two years later. My first love. A hunter killed her while trying to kill me during our wedding. The silk white dress she wore splattered with blood. I tried to use my magic to heal her but the bullet had hit her in the heart. She was dead before I could lay a hand on her. Right after she whispered 'I love you' for the last time. I hope she heard me say it back. I hope she knew I killed the bastard slowly, enjoying every second of it. What I would give to hear her voice again, see her glowing smile, her eyes twinkling, words can't explain. I loved how she would run into my arms every time she saw me with a beaming smile on her face. Forever is a long time to go without someone. I would know.

I snap out of my memory. The three of them break their heartfelt group hug. Holly's eyes are like shining stars of happiness. Colt grabs Abby's waist and kisses her. They kiss, hands going through hair, snogging. I should have stuck to the memory. How I killed him was beautiful. Holly walks up to me and catches me in an embrace. I wrench away. Holly's shoulders fall.

"I just want to thank you for saving Abby."

I nod. There is no reason for the embrace. I hate physical contact with anyone, the only time I get this close to someone is in a fight. I flick my fingers at the grass. Four glasses and a bottle of scotch appear where the body was. I didn't kill him with the blast. He is now back home in bed where this will have all been a dream. I sit down, pouring out the drinks. I top mine off with a dollop more. I need the drink. It has been a long day. The lovebirds' kiss breaks.

"Drinks." I wave them over.

"Drinks? Are you okay, Enzo?" Colt laughs.

"We're underage." Holly protests.

"Drink if you want. I'm not going to argue, more for me." I'm not forcing them. It's an offering. I know Abby will drink, she did at the party. I down my drink and go for another. I have a high tolerance. It'll be fine. I deserve it. At least that is what Alex texted me.

Silven

I open my eyes, grinning. I made it. To my surprise, I'm in a human bedroom, not the forest. How did I get here? Unless... the girl took back control of her own body. That's not possible! I should have full control the instant I enter her body. Doesn't matter. I have control now and she will not be getting it back. I jump from the bed, I go for the wardrobe to get out of the dog pyjamas. Why do humans like those creatures? They are soft and gentle. Why not get a wolf? Wolves are vicious animals yet loyal. I go through the clothes, she doesn't own any robes and very few items are black. I snatch up a shirt and a strange stretchy garment that seems awfully like thick tights. Both are black. I pull them on and walk out into a dark hallway. My human legs stumble, I curse. Humans are so inefficient. Hitting the wall, I knock a picture frame off the wall. The glass shatters. In the picture there are two girls, they look nothing alike but they both wear ridiculous hats reading 'It's my birthday'. They are twins. I'm inhabiting one of the twins.

"Abby, what are you doing?" A voice calls, a girl. My fingers itch for a kill. No. Not yet. I can't kill a family member yet.

"Abby?"

I turn, I am in Abby's body. "What?" I snap.

It is the girl from the photo, she looks a few years older than in the picture. "What are you doing?"

"Getting a drink." I roll my eyes.

"Fully dressed. Yeah right. Tell me the truth. You're seeing Colt, aren't you?"

Colt. He is Enzo's adopted brother or son. I'm not sure about their relationship, but I know Enzo would be crushed if Colt was killed. I smile, Abby is dating Colt. My minion did not disappoint.

"Yes. I am. Goodnight." I run down the rest of the steps.

"Wait. Do you have your phone?" The girl disappears into the bedroom and brings out a small rectangular device.

"Phone?"

"Yes, dummy." She tosses the thin device at me. I catch.

"You're welcome." She walks back to her room.

I store the fragile object in a bag I'd stolen from the dresser.

I waltz down the street, I remember phones, they existed before I was banished. They were large bricks that couldn't do much. I look at this one, a bright light flashes in my face. I sit on the bench, looking at the picture. It is Abby, her twin and three others. A boy and a girl, the boy is kissing the girl's cheek. The twin is receiving a peck on the cheek from another girl. Abby is the centre stage of the photo alone. The five of them are in some sort of park, swings behind them.

The phone begins to vibrate in my hand. It's going to explode. I drop it. I hear a crack, it lands face up. An old telephone sign pops up on the screen. It's a call, not a bomb. I pick the phone back up cautiously, and answer tapping the green telephone symbol.

"Hello, Abby?" The voice asks the other end of the phone.

"That's me," I speak into it.

"It's Enzo," Enzo is calling me, the bastard of Hell.

"Hello." My lips curl, my eyes catch someone, a jogger heading my way. Small buds in their ears. What noise are they trying to block? It doesn't matter to me, I can kill them. I mean if they are stupid enough to run alone at midnight it's their own fault really. I hold the kitchen knife in my hand, I will have to upgrade my weaponry. This is all the humans had in their house.

"I wanted to make sure you were okay," Enzo says. "Colt is worried and too afraid to call you."

"I have to go." I jab the red button. Enzo's voice cuts off. That is how you end a call. Good to know.

I rise from the bench. The jogger passes. I pounce, tackling her. My knife enters her chest. The swift ease of the kill is thrilling. I hear the blade crack a rib, it cuts through skin like paper. Howling, she whimpers under my grasp. Forcing down the blade again in joy, I plunge it into her heart. A final scream, blood splatters back onto my face. She is dead, her mouth gaping open. The soft gentle hazel eyes fade, they glaze over. The woman's body goes limp, her brain shutting down to nothingness.

The joy of the kill sends a chill down my spine. I sigh in pleasure. I haven't killed in years. It's beautiful. My knife goes into the corpse again. In and out, ruining the body. Satisfaction, running through my veins. Cutting up the body, laughing, the blood warm and bubbling on my fingertips. I slice open her chest, arms and face.

Hell's Daughter

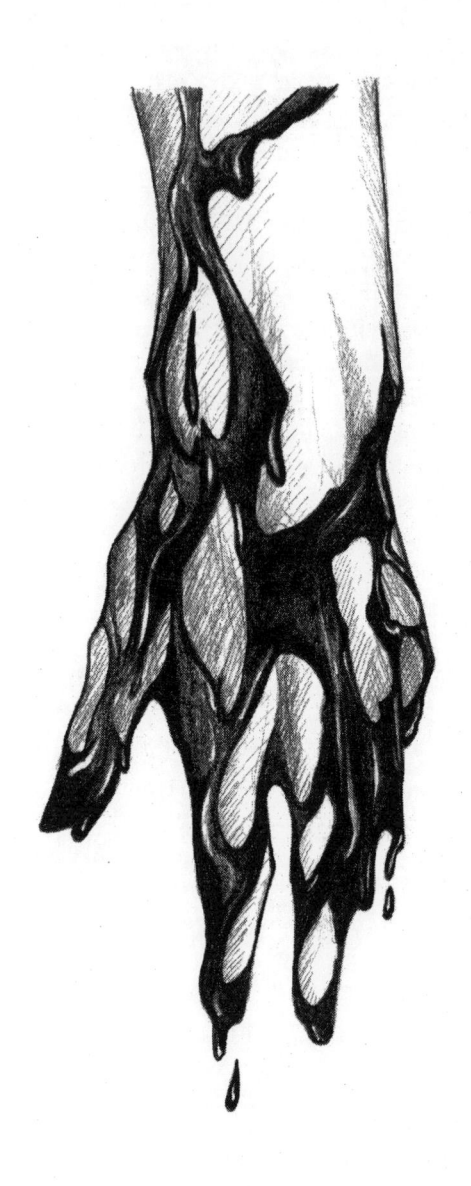

Slicing the flesh with long incisions blissfully, calming. The ghostly pale woman lies still, her lifeblood, mixing with grey sludgy intestines, all over the park. Her dead eyes hold a glassy doll look. Perfection.

I lean in to whisper in her ear. "One down thirty-five more to go."

I chuckle, the silver blade touches her cheek, scratching it gently. I'll enjoy the next one more. A little torture while they are alive. I'll get them to beg a few times. Then kill them. Now where to stash the bodies. There must be a good spot to hide them for a while. I wave my hand, the body floats above the ground following me away from the city. I'll find somewhere.

Wandering down the dark alleyways my eyes dart to the lampposts, cameras perch among them. There are many more than when I last visited Earth. A whisk of my hand and leaves flutter away blocking the view of cameras. The night is dead, not a person or car in sight. The city is small, we are near a forest, I can smell it. I skip down the road of freedom. I love Hell, it is exquisite, I could run down that plain for hours. I never got bored down there. I would venture to Earth for some mischief at my own leisure. Lucifer was the ultimate ruler. The pleasure I got from leading attacks and murdering who I pleased. I miss it all. Before Lucifer was defeated, we were planning to conquer Heaven. We were going to kill all the angels and take ownership. We will get there one day, we have eternity.

Finally, I find a beautiful cave in the middle of the forest, deep enough no human will come close. It's safe here. I tuck the bodies inside. I picked up a few on the way. A few lonely drunks wandering the streets. The cave is a decent size, I won't need to relocate. The city here has plenty of people to kill but at the outskirts, there is ample space in the forest to hide the corpses.

My hands begin to shake and my eyes begin to roll back. Clenching my fist, what is going on? Fighting back, my eyes struggle to focus. I struggle to hold onto one the dead woman's

Hell's Daughter

arm. I'm losing control. The stupid human is fighting back. They aren't meant to be able to do that. My legs tremble. There is no time. I spin, running out the cave while I still can. My eyes refuse to focus on the trees while I stumble aimlessly through the woodland. Sprinting, I use the air to carry my body away. The power falters while I struggle to remain in control. My mission can't end before it starts. If Alex finds out about it, that is game over. I'll be back in Hell for my execution and Lucifer will never be able to take back his throne. My eyes droop. I drop to the ground, my powers giving in. No. I need to…

Abby

Waking up, I roll out of bed. My hand strokes soft grass strands. Jolting up, my eyes flash open. I'm in a forest. The city lights and car horns blare in the distance. A soft orange glow beams down from the sky. How did I get here? The last thing I remember is collapsing in bed. I am wearing clothes, not pyjamas. Staring down at my hands, I see dry blood, flaking off my fingers. My heart threatens to burst out of my chest. What is going on? There is no sign of anyone else. My clothes are stained with a mixture of blood and mud. Scanning my body, I find an injury. A gash on my arm steadily bleeds which explains the blood. How did I get it? I got quite drunk last night but Enzo sobered us up before we went home. I scramble for my pocket, with luck I find my phone. Grasping it, I take a deep breath. I have my phone. No messages. It's four am. I have time to get home and pretend it never happened. It could be a side effect of being resurrected from the dead. Enzo told me I'd died. He brought me back to life. Those facts haven't quite sunk in yet. I'll talk to him about it, alone. Enzo made me swear not to tell anyone. I try to keep my breathing steady. Enzo will know what to do. Even if I want to contact the others I can't. I couldn't tell if Enzo was joking about Alex killing me. I don't dare risk it.

I call Enzo. He answers at the first ring. Thank god.

"Hello? Abby. I gave you my number. No correction, Colt gave you my number for emergencies or when he wants me to contact you for him. It better be important."

"Sorry for waking you."

A snort. "I've been up for two hours already. What is so important that you needed to call me not Colt."

"I'm lost."

"So? Colt could find you."

I bite my tongue, I'm terrified and Enzo is being an asshole.

"I don't know where I am. I'm bleeding. I'm in the middle of a fucking forest. I don't know how I got here. I think it could be a side effect of being resurrected which is why I contacted you." I ramble.

The line is quiet at the other end. I hear a crash.

"Enzo? Enzo?" I call angrily, shaking my phone. I notice the battery life, I have one percent left. "Enzo!" I yell before it dies.

I lose contact, and I don't know if he is coming to help. I feel dizzy, there is a large quantity of blood on my clothes. I shiver in the cold air, autumn leaves crunch under my boots.

"Hello." A voice declares.

I spin. "Holy shit, Enzo!"

Wordlessly, he grabs my arm and surges magic through the wound. How did he know where I was? I know he can teleport to places but to people? I relax, the pain from my arm leaving.

"Thanks."

"It's not an effect of the blood. It cures everyone. That's the point."

"I never used to sleepwalk." I protest. "How did you find me?"

"Magic." He shrugs.

"Really? You can track people like that?"

"No. I searched the entire forest for your scent between portaling around methodically till I found you."

"Wow!" I exclaim, impressed.

"That's called sarcasm."

I chuckle, I should know Enzo wouldn't put that much effort in to find me. Enzo shoulders are tense, letting go of my healed arm.

"What's wrong?" I glance at his defensive stature.

"Nothing. I need your shirt."

"What?"

"It's easier to track someone with something they own. I'll need it if you get lost again."

"Can't I give you another shirt?" I am willing to give him a shirt but I am currently wearing this one.

"The blood on the shirt. It increases its strength. I will get you another shirt."

I guess that makes sense. I would rather not bleed over another shirt for him. Besides, this isn't my favourite shirt.

"Sure. Can you take me home first?"

Enzo waggles his fingers in an artistic flourish. "I will but you have to come to my home first. I need to run some tests. We can see if I can find out why you are sleepwalking."

"Okay."

Teleporting to a room, I stare in awe. This is unlike any room in the house I've seen. The room is bare except for a few practical things. The entire room is spotless. The bedsheets without a crease, it is like no-one ever sleeps on it. There aren't any empty glasses of water, mugs or food wrappers. It is like a ghost lives in this room, there is no sign of cobwebs or dust. Enzo's room. A fresh pair of clothes on the bed.

"I need a shower." I refer to the blood and drying mud on my skin.

"That way." Enzo points to a door.

I scoop up the clothes, including the shoes. There is no imprint on the bed where they sat.

The bathroom, it is exactly the same as the bedroom. It is practical with no personal decoration. Bottles of shampoo and body wash sit on the side, ginger, orange and sandalwood. At that moment, new bottles spark onto the shelf. Coconut shampoo and conditioner sit there along with a passion fruit body wash. I guess those are for me. I lay the clothes on the rack next to one of the fresh and fluffy new towels.

I start the shower, the water is the perfect temperature. No doubt it is magic. No shower is naturally this good. Normal showers take at least a minute to adjust to a good temperature. The dry blood drips off my skin, flaking away down the drain. What happened last night? I wish I knew but I don't remember anything. I wrack my brain for answers, for a sliver of information explaining why I was there. Rubbing my face, I clean away the cake of mud staining my skin. I shudder.

CHAPTER EIGHT

Enzo

Pulling on my shoes for my morning run, my phone rings. I answer the call from Abby, I don't understand why she would call me over Colt. He cares about her more than I do. I would know, he spent two hours mooning over her last night. Sadly, Colt is a hopeless romantic. I guess everyone has their flaws. My ears perk up when she mentions she is hurt. That catches my attention. I leave the phone and race to get her. I can't let her die, that is one thing I refuse to do. Colt, Abby and Holly are all under my protection. They came under my protection, the second Colt fell for Abby. I will protect them with my life. I would never let Colt suffer the pain of losing someone he cares about like I did.

In three seconds, I find her. I didn't spare any time. I have her, she bleeds from a gash in her arm. Hardly serious, I grab her arm and begin to work.

"Enzo!" She squeals in a mixture of surprise and relief.

I tense. She is covered in blood, but it isn't hers. I can smell the different scents of the blood, there is a minimum of three other people's blood on the shirt. Looking closer, there are intestines on her jeans. She hasn't noticed. She jabbers on, I respond in kind, I reassure her it wasn't because of the resurrection. My mind races, something isn't right about her. I ask for her shirt. I sigh when she asks why. Abby asks too many questions, but I know that. Prepared, I lie to her, telling her that her blood will enhance my sensing. She'll never know I lied.

Returning home to my bedroom, I ask to do some tests. Abby thinks it's to help her sleepwalking. It's not. I need to test a theory. I pray I'm wrong. It's why I need the shirt. Thankfully, Abby asks for a shower. That will give me twenty minutes. She gives up her shirt and leaves to wash up.

Clutching the shirt, I close my eyes. I smell it. Definitely not her blood... It's about three hours old. From the amount of the blood, it suggests the person is at least unconscious and possibly dead. I multiply that by three, at least three different scents, all human. This shirt will be useful if it's what I think.

Twenty minutes later, I sit Abby on the desk chair. My hands' scan for demonic energy. I search her entire body. The magic I emit is purple, it turns to maroon on contact. I am correct, her entire body gives off demon energy. Shit. Abby is possessed. A demon is in her head. This isn't Abby. Yet no demon is smart enough to plan and know how to act like the human they possess. Normally they take the body and go.

"Do you remember our phone call last night?"

"No."

I nod, scanning again. The demon energy reading falls lower. No demon can mask their presence. The energy seems to pulse, focusing on her brain. The energy is faint through the rest of her body. I need to know if this is Abby or a demon. If it is a demon, then I will have to find out what to do with it. It's easy to tell. "When was your and Colt's first kiss. Give details."

"What?" Abby exclaims in surprise.

"Answer the question." Demons don't get memories from the person they take over. Abby will be the only one able to answer this.

"Okay. We were at Colt's party, we were making out. Colt's bite my lower lip and then Selena came out of the forest screaming."

That checks out. She still has demonic energy in her veins which suggests something is there and I need to solve it. A human can rarely fight off the possession of a demon.

"I'll see what I can do about your sleepwalking." I promise. I'll follow her tonight if she sleepwalks. I will see what she does. If a demon is possessing her, it'll be a problem.

"Thanks. Did I catch you at a bad time?" Abby changes the subject. "You're a bit underdressed."

I'm wearing a pair of baggy joggers and a plain shirt with old scruffy trainers. I wear them to work out in. I snap my fingers, the outfit changes. I wear a button-up shirt, jeans and smart boots.

"Better?"

"I wasn't complaining."

She defends herself, acting like I changed my outfit for her. I didn't. This is what I would wear after the jog which I didn't get this morning.

"Downstairs Colt will be eating breakfast by now. You are welcome to join him."

"At this time?"

I sigh. "Vampires are nocturnal. He sleeps for a few hours a day. By the way, stay away from his food, the main ingredient is blood."

"Thanks, I'll do that and thanks for the rescue. I appreciate it."

"Your welcome."

I don't normally receive 'thank yous'. Abby wraps her arms around my body. I hesitate, I resist the urge to flinch away. I pat her awkwardly before pushing back.

"Go eat."

She nods slowly. "I will."

I watch her leave. I need Alex's help. If a demon is possessing Abby, I need her advice on how to diminish it while keeping Abby alive. I will try and save her but there is a chance I won't be able to. It's unheard of purging demons from the human body. The only person who knows more than I do about the supernatural is Alex. If she can't help, then my last resort will be to kill her.

Abby

Skipping downstairs, I feel oddly well after the amazing shower. In the kitchen, there are plates in the sink and crumbs on the sideboard. It actually looks like people live down here. The wallpaper is modern, paintings of retro squares on the wall. There are hardly any cooking tools, there is no block of knives, pots or pans hanging on the wall. I assume Enzo can cook without any equipment.

Colt is in sweats sitting at the table eating a bowl of cereal swimming in blood.

"Gross." I announce.

"Hey." Colt turns, waving to a plate of breakfast.

"How did you know I was here?"

Colt taps his ear.

"From upstairs?"

A laugh. "Yes, and Enzo told me."

I roll my eyes, I survey my options. There are many different cereals, types of bread, pastries and more. My stomach growls. Colt slurps from the bowl. I laugh, blood around his lips. The bowl is left empty. A glass jug of blood for Colt. He takes a pastry and pours blood on top. It looks disgusting. I take a plate and help myself.

"So, what are you doing here?" Colt raises an eyebrow.

"Umm--"

Hell's Daughter

"Let me guess. You sleepwalked in the forest and called Enzo instead of me."

"How…" I remember his vampire hearing. That is how.

"Vampire hearing. We are meant to be very untrusting creatures. We have special ears to hear everything being plotted against us." Colt chuckles.

"You are nothing like that."

"No. I'm not. I can still be a little offended you called him not me."

"I thought it was a side effect of the magic and almost dying. I assumed he would be the expert. Then my phone died." I explain.

Colt smiles. "Ah, you're right there."

"I'll call you next time." I bite into the croissant. My mouth waters. "Damn this tastes good."

"Enzo made it, he likes to cook. Have you called Holly yet, let her know you are okay?"

"No. My phone died, can I borrow yours?"

"Check it now."

I look at it. It is fully charged.

"How? Enzo." I answer my own question. Magic seems like an amazing power to have. I call Holly, it takes to the seventh ring.

"Abby?" She croaks.

"Hi." It is only six in the morning, I bet she just woke up. She probably hasn't noticed I'm gone. "I just wanted to tell you I'm with Colt and Enzo so I'll see you at school."

"I know."

"You know?" I frown, how does she know that? Werewolf hearing can't be that good, we are a half-an-hour drive away.

"You told me."

"When?"

"Last night, I caught you sneaking out. You said you were meeting Colt, don't you remember?"

"Yes." I lie. "Sorry, I totally forgot. Bye." I hang up. "Apparently, I came to see you last night."

"You never got here if you did."

The click of a coffee pot sends me spinning. Enzo is on the phone and pouring out a cup of coffee. His footsteps don't make a sound.

"You said you don't remember our call which puts your sleepwalking between one and four am."

"What did we speak about?" I ask out of curiosity.

"Doesn't matter."

Colt sighs. "Don't be so mean, we all know you like Abby really."

Enzo chuckles. "I'd hope so, I saved her life if you don't remember. Therefore, I'm not mean, just myself."

Colt rolls his eyes. "Fine, brood away."

"I will." Enzo smiles, putting down the coffee cup. "I'll be back later, have fun at school."

Enzo waltzes away out the back door which leads to a wonderful large garden. The house must sit on an acre of land. I don't know where the house stops and the forest begins.

"Do you want to go to school today?" Colt asks. "If you don't want to go, I'll stay back with you."

"No, I'm fine. Thank you for helping yesterday."

"Your welcome, Enzo did most of the work."

"Yes, but we both know he was only there because of you." I ease closer to him.

He smiles. "Well, I can take credit for that."

He leans in for a kiss. Electricity burst through my veins. His lips are hungry on mine. I bring him in, closer. Colt grins against my lips. I can taste the blood he just ate on his lips.

Holly met us at the school this morning. The day is long, the lessons feel even longer than they really are. I don't pay much attention. I am on my phone under the desk. I research causes of sleepwalking, Enzo said he would look into it. But it cannot be supernatural. It is recorded that a near-death experience can cause problems sleeping. It suggests visiting a doctor or taking sleeping pills. I can't do either. I feel drowsy, but I fight falling asleep. I don't have lessons with either Colt or Holly today. Enzo doesn't seem worried about Holly being alone today.

"Abby." Kyle nudges me.

I put away my phone quickly. "Hmmm? Yeah."

I look up to the board, I have no idea what is going on. Notes fill Kyle's notebook and my page is blank.

"Are you okay?" Kyle asks.

I nod, picking up my pen, I'm not going to write anything.

"Do you want to hang out after the lesson, there is a new cafe nearby. Lily is desperate for you to try it." Kyle offers.

I shake my head. "No thanks. I have plans."

Kyle smirks. "What with your new boyfriend. Colt, right? I saw you making out at the party."

"Yeah." I will be seeing Colt but not for the reason he thinks.

"We should all go out at some point. We can make it a triple date."

I frown. "You went on double dates without me?"

Kyle curses, I laugh. I know they did, Holly can't keep a secret. They have been on many double dates and left me out. I often have fifth wheeled on dates. "It's fine, I knew."

"Thank god." Kyle chuckles. "Is that a yes to the triple date?"

"One day." I offer, I don't promise. I don't know when there'll be a chance.

Enzo

Jumping through, I enter the portal to Hell. The horrible dusty grey portal disappears behind me. All my bones snap, one after the other. Fire burns in my veins. My body shakes violently, a snout, paws and sharp teeth appear. In a second, the entire world flips on its axis. The green trees, soft grass, gentle sun are a myth in Hell. The cool breeze is replaced with a sharp wind, ruffling my fur. The scorching heat is attempting to drown me. Why do I have fur? Why does any demonic creature have fur? I will never understand. Hell is the hottest dimension to exist. Slowly, my blood temperature rises and the foul heat subsides. The pressing weight of the air pressure fades. Someone without hell blood wouldn't survive more than five minutes, a mortal would die the second they entered the portal.

I can only be here in my Hellhound form unless Alex administers the power for me to do otherwise. I need to find her. If a demon is possessing Abby, she should know which demon it is. Demons taking over human bodies without her permission is grounds for punishment by death. The blazing buildings of fire roar. Hell is an endless land of ravines and lava then, if you can reach the other side, it is cold and dead. Yet, it has improved since Alex took charge. Demons' homes aren't caves or holes in the mud. There are structures that could be considered houses. Hell could never be like Earth. Demons would never accept it if it were, most don't like Alex's improvements. None of them would dare say, they are too frightened of her. There are a few demons, who are loyal to Lucifer despite the fact they are beasts of the underworld.

When Alex first took over she hired me for protection. There was uproar, Hell has never changed its ruler. Lucifer was made to rule it. The original demon. Till Alex. It didn't take long for most to bow down, once they realised they wouldn't win. Lucifer's loyal followers live in the cells in the deepest part of the prison. Silven the accomplice who has never given up on him sits in the deepest. I had to take care of her. She attempted to murder Alex and her family.

My eyes dart around, it's quiet. Too quiet. A few demons lurk in the sky, a few in the shadows but not swarms of them. I pad along the dry rough dirt to the palace.

Hell's Daughter

Alex lives on Earth, but she made sure her Hell home is the best there is. Alex would not be seen with less than the best. The black rock, tall and majestic. The building is huge and in much better condition than when Lucifer owned it. My feet singe on the dirt, leaving burnt paw prints.

Strolling into the palace, I enter the throne room. I howl. Alex isn't on the throne. I circle the room, the throne is made of polished hell oak, plush demonic leather, blood rubies enlaced with black diamonds over the throne head. I have never seen Alex in a crown. I'm sure she has one. Bones decorate the armrests. The bones of creatures that belong here. It used to be Lucifer's throne, Alex has never changed it. She likes knowing she took his place, it symbolises her power over Lucifer.

A few moments pass, Alex is nowhere to be seen. I wander through the castle, trying to find her. Most of the rooms are large and empty, Alex doesn't have much use for the castle. She goes between two chambers, the bedroom and the throne room. She isn't on Earth otherwise I would have been able to contact her. She could be in Heaven. I highly doubt it. She went once and vowed never to go again. She called the angels selfish, self-righteous, stuck-up bastards. I sigh, Alex isn't here. I would have found her otherwise. I scrawl a message in the dirt in the throne room. I sign my name with a paw-print, she'll recognise it. None of the demons will try and wipe out the message. They wouldn't dare.

I frightened many demons when I worked down here. I lived here for the duration of my job. Technically, Hell is my home as much as Earth, is but I never see it like that. I spent three months in Hell. The food here is foul, there is barely anywhere to grow real food. I used magic to get all my meals. I worked for Alex not because I needed money, I worked for free. I worked because I knew she would be a good ruler for Hell. I like Alex because she has the same morals as I do. I spent most of my time by her side, being a bodyguard of sorts. Alex would joke it was to symbolise power, that I was a trophy by her side. I am notorious for being difficult and blood-thirsty for revenge, yet she got me to be her bodyguard. I smile softly to myself and leave the empty castle.

Pulling on my clothes, I know that visit went badly. No answers at all. My phone is empty, not a message. Alex hasn't seen the message yet. Colt and the other two will be back soon. Colt said they would all be back by three. I'll study, I have plenty of books. I'll read about possession. My phone buzzes, it's the news. Five people went missing yesterday. Nothing is caught on the city cameras, they were conveniently blocked. The missing people are from this area. I check for the time of the disappearances. It is suspected that they went missing between midnight and five this morning. This isn't looking good for Abby.

Hours later, I have nothing. The three of them return from school. They look tired and fed up. Backpacks drop onto my pristine floor the second they enter my door. I have coat hangers for a reason. Is it that hard to lift a bag? I whisk a hand, the bags put themselves up on the hangers. They slump on the sofa, in discussion with each other. Jackets are thrown off and left on my couch and their shoes go up on the seat. I have suddenly become the father of three grouchy teenagers. I did not ask for this. I sigh. What? Am I meant to give them cookies and milk? I walk into my living room, they don't care to notice. I cough, loudly. The group looks up collectively.

"Holly needs training. Come on." I usher them away from the sofa.

They glare, none of them want to move. They've hardly had a bad day. Except for Abby possibly, her morning was a little shitty. I herd them off to the garden for some martial arts. Alcohol might be a good way to improve their spirits, but I don't think it's the most responsible solution.

CHAPTER NINE

Silven

Waking, I curse. It is nightfall again, I can only control her when she is asleep. Most would be impressed she can fight off a demon of my standing. I should be too powerful for her, this does put a spanner in the works. I can't have her finding my ritual site and ruining my plan. I doubt the girl suspected the truth when she woke up in the forest. Probably thought it was a prank or she was sleepwalking. I hope she didn't tell her friends. I don't want Enzo finding out, he's the only one smart enough to work it out. I don't remember how far I got before she gained control.

I take her phone from the nightstand. I change, the clothes I wore are no longer in the wardrobe. I dress in a dark outfit and tip-toe out the door. I need to find ten more people tonight and a car. Cars have gotten bigger since I was last on Earth. I will be able to fit a few more bodies in the boot. Carrying is too much effort, I need to preserve my energy for the murders. It's a cool night, the half-moon lit above. Walking down the street, I spot a large vehicle. It reads 'hire-a-van' on the side. Skipping over in joy, this is big with plenty of boot space. My finger's snap and the door unlocks. Jumping up onto the driver's seat, they have been updated since I was up here. I press a small red button, the engine revs. There used to be keys for that. I grab the wheel, driving isn't something I'm an expert on. I release the handbrake. I slam on the pedal. The van vaults forward, smacking the car in front causing an alarm to start.

I sigh, the alarm stops at my will.

"Hey! That's my van!" A man, face as red as a robin's breast pounds the window with a fat fist.

Casually, I roll down the window. "Excuse me?"

"This is my van, bitch."

I have found my first kill of the night. I lean out the window and catch the poor excuse of a man with a punch. A stifled scream and he bends over in pain holding his nose.

I laugh. The power, authority and sweet lingering smell of fear waft in the air. All of which I've missed dearly. My words hiss. "You. Will. Die. Tonight."

The icy glare in the old man's eyes fades and switches to fear. I chuckle, hands sliding around his neck easily. A chill runs down my spine, excitement thumping through my human veins. My grip slowly drains the life out of him, second by second. Pointlessly, he flails against the van door, trying to fight back. I could make this much quicker with a sharp snap of the neck. I prefer to watch every hope, dream and struggle fade. The will to live failing. The man stops moving. Veins stick out his forehead, striving to get oxygen but they don't. Dead as a dodo. I love that human saying. Two minutes pass, I drop him, a ring of purple bruises forming around his chunky neck. Dead on the pavement, he lies limp as a rag doll. Opening the door, I just miss the body. The wind carries him to the back of the van, I fling the doors open. He lies there, lifeless, in the empty dirty van. One down, nine to go. Time to get back on the road. I start the engine and send the car rocketing up the street, pressing harder on the accelerator, two hands tightly on the wheel. I click the button, the radio begins to play. I hum along to the new songs, humans do have an interesting style of music.

My window rolls down to the sound of drunk teenagers singing, there are two voices. One female and the other male. They giggle at nothing, barely able to stand. I should help them sober up. The street is clear. I pull the van over, or try to. The vehicle scratches two others on its way. I hit the pavement, roaring up onto it. The couple run fearfully in the opposite direction. I cackle, heading right for them. The engine growls the harder, I press on the accelerator. The two connect with the bonnet, crashing into the windshield. I hear them cry out for help, over the sound of their bones crunching. At this rate I may get more than ten sacrifices tonight.

"Stop!"

A little voice howls. Looking up, a little girl with a furious scowl on her face, yells from her bedroom window. Her eyes fall to the already dead bodies, they have no hope of surviving. At least I have a new candidate to be a sacrifice.

Enzo

I wake up from my nap. It's eleven. I forced Holly and Abby to go home early. They should be asleep by now. If I'm correct the demon will be in control now. I magic on clothes I pick trainers, jeans, a plain shirt and a leather jacket. I comb my hair and brush my teeth. I drink a mug of coffee, I will need it to stay awake. I phone Abby. There is no reply. I create a portal, I need to check if Abby is still at home asleep or out as a demon.

Portaling, I land in Abby's family kitchen. It is a mess, dirty plates piling high. Their parents don't appear to be home much, Abby and Holly stay out late and do as they please. I never see them check with their parents about it. I walk up the creaky stairs. There are three closed doors and one wide open. I move to the open door, there are clothes all over the floor. Abby's room. The bed is empty and the phone is gone. Shit. Immediately, I portal back home.

I pound up the stairs, I will need help. Colt will be the best for it.

"Colt! Wake up!" I knock on his door.

"I didn't oversleep, did I?" Colt groans.

I open the door. "Get dressed! We have to go."

"Where?" Colt grabs his phone. "It's midnight. You know I sleep from eleven pm to four am."

"It's to do with Abby."

Those five words have him out of bed and racing for a shirt and jeans. I grin to myself.

"What is it?"

"She may be possessed."

Colt stops, shirt around his shoulders, he doesn't seem to care I am still in the room. "What?"

"She didn't sleepwalk. She was covered in another human's blood. Multiple if I'm correct."

I chuck the old shirt at him. "A little maybe hers but not all of it."

Colt smells the shirt and nods. He looks terrified.

"Now. Come on. She is up again. We need to find the demon."

"Does Abby know?" He asks.

"No."

"Good."

My eyes widen in surprise, I wasn't expecting that to be his response. I thought he would be mad. "We need to find her."

He puts on shoes and a jacket. "Why didn't you tell me earlier?"

"In case you told her." I sigh. "Get in the car."

"The car?" Admittedly, we don't often take the car, teleportation is easier.

"Yes, I don't know where she is. We'll drive around looking for something. My magic isn't picking up anything."

"The demon is stopping your tracking."

"Yes, car now!"

We run to the garage to the McLaren. I swing into the driver's seat.

I chuck the shirt to Colt. "Use that."

I start the engine, it roars to life. My foot steps on the accelerator. I rev the car down the road. The garage door shuts itself on our way out. Colt swings his head out the window. Vampires can smell blood, to them everyone's blood is different. They can tell quality, blood type, which is heavy in iron, which has high or low cholesterol. Hounds and Werewolves are more expert at people's unique scent. Colt's fangs hang from his mouth.

I take the shirt back with one hand. I sniff it. It smells like her under all the blood. Abby smells flowery quite like roses. It reminds me of an old friend I lost, only she smelled more strongly of daisies. I swing the car to the right, there are a few other scents in the air, but I can pick Abby's out. It's faint but definitely there. It's a windy night, allowing scents to spread. It is difficult to pinpoint a location.

I chuck the shirt back to Colt. The car slides around a corner at seventy miles an hour. I guess I should slow down.

"What do we do once we find her?" Colt asks. "Can you free someone of demonic possession?"

I was hoping he wouldn't ask that question.

"Is it curable?" He continues.

I hesitate, I should tell him the truth. "I don't know a cure."

"What?"

"I went to find Alex but she isn't in Hell. I'm sure we'll find a way."

I lie. I'm not sure there is a way.

"What normally happens?"

"You kill them and free their soul," I reply honestly if I have to do it, he needs to know.

A curse, a string of swear words. Some new and inventive, some not so much. It stops for a moment. "Wait. Callum was he…"

"No. He was being controlled, it's different."

"We killed an innocent person!" The car shakes, a dent in my dashboard. That is an understatement, there is a hole in my dashboard.

"No. We didn't. I fixed him up, he is recovering at home none the wiser of what happened last night."

I snap my fingers to fix the dashboard.

"You saved him?" Colt sounds genuinely surprised.

I don't kill innocent people, I stand by that. I will forever. Callum was innocent, the demon was controlling him. The demon will pay but Callum won't. A car alarm blasts. Chances are that is our demon. I spin the car around in the direction of the siren.

Racing up the road, a van comes soaring around a corner of the road. Whoever is driving doesn't know the first thing about steering. The van charges our way. I swerve, the van rushes by. I glance at the driver. This isn't a drunk driver, it's Abby. I see the evil glint in her eyes suggesting that something is not quite human. I turn the car around in pursuit. I charge the car forward. I flip the car into sports mode. Gripping the wheel tightly, the vibrations of the engine flooding the car as I drive dangerously through the streets. With a snap of my fingers, all the circuits in the speed cameras go down. The van gets closer, it swerves down streets but I am quick to follow. The demon doesn't know its way around the city, meaning I have the upperhand. I shift up gears swiftly. I dart out a car's way, a loud horn blows. Colt undoes his seatbelt.

"Are you mad?" I ask in disbelief. "You may be a vampire, but you aren't invisible. If we crash…"

"I'm going to try and jump on the roof. Get me closer."

"Bloody hell," I mutter under my breath.

There is no stopping Colt, the window is already down and he's climbing out. The demon is steering through the middle of the street, I can't get next to it. Ahead there is an intersection, it'll give me the chance to catch up. The van speeds past the red light straight across the intersection. I swerve to the right, going around the side of the van. The tyres screech, I drove professionally many years ago. I know what I'm doing, thankfully. I steer forward, till we are neck and neck on the road.

Colt clutches the roof for support while he hangs halfway out the window. The van moves our way, ready to crush Colt. He jumps, grabbing the bike rack at the top of the van and climbing on top. The van smashes into the side of my McLaren. The car shakes, I steady it and shove right back. We collide again. A human walks across the road in front, neither of us has our lights on. He can't see us, I wouldn't be able to see him without night vision. Shit. The demon won't stop for him. Moving away from the van, I push the pedal harder to build momentum. Yanking the wheel, the tyres spin, slamming the McLaren, into the van with incredible force. The front of the car connects with the backside panel of the van, pushing the demon further off the road, we are only a few feet away. The human sees, and runs, barely missing the van. Holy shit, that was close.

In my brief moment of distraction, the van speeds up. My car jumps forward, the van lurching out the way. Spinning off-road I slam on the brakes hard, I hear them shriek in a desperate attempt to try and divert it. The car sails into a tree. The windshield shatters on impact. I pull up my arms to shield my face as I go through it. Smacking the tree, I groan in agony. So much for a seatbelt and airbags. My car is toast. No fire but the faint smell of burning. The front is crumpled like paper. Blood pours down my face, my clothes are ripped. Chunks of glass stick out my forearms and a shard through my cheek. Rolling off the top of my car, I thump to the ground. I wince in agony. Ripping the shards out I hiss, the one in my cheek cuts a hole through to the inside of my mouth.

I shred the trench coat and sweater. I can't teleport to the van, I can only teleport to a space, not an object. The van is moving so I won't be able to time it right. I would land on the road. I need to turn into a Hellhound if I want to catch up. I growl, doubling over. My back cracks, my stance shrinking to the form of a muscular Hellhound.

Charging, I chase them. I can't see them anymore. Tomorrow I am tying Abby up with very strong restraints. Flames blaze off my body, I dart between lamp posts. I can already feel my body healing, the wounds patching up and scabbing over. The throbbing pain in my head is going numb. A voice calls out my name.

"Enzo!" I skid to a stop. "Enzo!" Colt stumbles out of a bush, looking terrified. "I lost her- I got thrown off."

I gruff a reply.

"Bodies. She has bodies in the back. Ten, I think. Enzo." Colt's lips tremble, his eyes dilating probably a concussion. He was thrown hard from a moving vehicle.

"There was a kid. A kid! Don't demons have any limits?" Tears brim in his eyes. I nuzzle his legs comfortingly. Colt hates murder. "We have to stop it," Colt swears. "We have to try and find her."

I nod in agreement.

We stop, the sun is beginning to rise. We've spent hours searching. There is nothing. The demon has disappeared into thin air. I never knew it would be that easy to hide a van. We have been trying to track the demon for hours using all the techniques we can think of, but the demon isn't stupid. It has thrown off the scent. Colt's nails are bitten to the quick where he has been chewing them all night. We need to call Alex. She can find out what is happening. No way she doesn't know a demon is missing. Especially if it's smart enough to block tracking. This is a demon of a high ranking. Colt's phone rings.

"Abby." He whispers.

Finally, she is her again, I've been waiting. Her scent starts to catch wind again. She is her again.

CHAPTER TEN

Abby

My back is ice cold. What am I sleeping on? My fingers touch cold metal, my eyes flash open. It's pitch black. My hands feel a long scratch like dents on the metal. Squinting, I see metal walls. My heartbeat races, jumping to my feet my head touches the ceiling. I groan, also metal. I feel the walls, I'm in the back of a van. Scrambling in the dim light, I go in the direction of what I think is the door. I slip on a liquid, head bumping the doors frantically. They fling open, the sunlight hits my face. I'm soaked in blood from head to toe. My clothes are torn, my hair is a mess with knots. The van is a blood bath. This can't all be mine. I would be dead tenfold. Grabbing my phone, which is safely tucked in my pocket. I call Colt in a frenzy. His name is next to Holly's in my speed dial.

"Where are you?" He asks immediately.

I take a deep breath. "I'm not sure." I circle the van.

The bonnet is open, it is singed and the engine is melted. I gulp. The engine has been on fire. A bark yaps in the background of the call.

"We'll be there in ten." Colt hangs up.

"But…" I trail off, shuddering at the sight of the van. What happened here? How did I get here? I don't remember anything. A howl comes through the trees. The trees around me are bare. The dead leaves scatter on the ground even though it is the middle of summer. I climb a sturdy tree in search of Colt and Enzo. I grab the firm branches one by one scaling the tree like a cat. Over the dead trees, I see normal summer ones, with luscious green leaves on healthy oak wood. This isn't normal. Staring out over the trees I can't see Enzo and Colt. Another howl.

"Hello." Colt zips out of no-where.

Vaulting back in surprise, I lose my footing and tumble out of the tree. Dashing forward, Colt gracefully catches me in his arms. I laugh, I peck his cheek and drop out of his arms. I didn't doubt they wouldn't be able to find me. Colt looks worn out and his clothes are dirty.

A snort, Enzo circles the van. He isn't human, but a Hellhound.

"We've been searching for you all night." Colt smiles weakly.

"All night?"

"Yes, do you remember anything?"

I shake my head. "No."

Enzo pounces into the back of the van, venturing inside.

"There is a lot of blood, I don't know where it's from."

Something isn't adding up here. This can't be normal. This blood can't be mine, I'm positive of it. I'm not hurt.

"Looks like an abandoned van, you probably just found it. It doesn't look like it has been driven anywhere." Colt examines the crushed engine.

I agree it's a miracle that any van even found its way in the forest. I can't see how it could have been driven here, would have to fly or something which isn't possible, I think.

"You think so?" His words are reassuring.

"You have nothing to do with this." He points to the van.

Hell's Daughter

"Why did I sleepwalk all the way here?" I ask. "Nothing supernatural is it?"

"Possibly," Colt admits, his face is distraught, suggesting there is more to know.

"You'll tell me if there is anything else, right?"

"Yes. Of course. Definitely." Colt nods.

I smile, a small ounce of tension relieving from my body. "Thank you. I know I can trust you."

A simple nod. "You aren't hurt, are you?"

"No."

"Holly will be up soon, for her morning training session. Are you coming with us or do you need to sleep?"

"I'm coming." I insist. I cannot not be there for Holly.

"Good, it'll be more interesting with you there." Colt eases into a smile, leaning in a little closer.

"Do you remember our first kiss?" He whispers.

"At the party," I state.

His shoulders relax and he grins and nods. I lean in for a kiss, Colt hesitates before kissing me back. His hand holds the back of my neck, keeping me close. My heart beats faster in my chest, my fears washing away.

A cough from behind us. "Break it up!"

I roll my eyes, but I pull away reluctantly. Enzo, who is human now, waves a hand to create a portal. "You two get Holly and go home for training. I'll catch up."

"What are you going to do?" I ask.

"Does it matter?" Enzo scrunches up his nose.

I take that as he isn't going to tell me. I thought Enzo and I were finally getting along. I am really stupid to think Enzo would stay unguarded and nice for long. Colt smiles taking my hand and we fly through the portal leaving Enzo behind.

In my bedroom, I grab a fresh change of clothes, the ones I currently wear are stained in mud. "I'll wait downstairs." Colt disappears out the door, closing it behind him.

I put on a cropped sweater, jeans and ankle boots. I brush my hair, it is in a tangled mess, I pull out a few leaves. What was I doing? Taking a deep breath, I stare in the mirror. Trying to remember, my hands wrack through the tangle-free hair. My brain remains empty as if I slept dreamlessly all night. I curse. I must sleepwalk for a reason. I have to figure it out. I used to sleepwalk as a child, but I haven't in the last ten years. Why would I start again now? More importantly, why am I visiting abandoned vans?

Enzo

My phone goes straight to voicemail. Damn Alex! Why isn't she returning my calls? This has never happened before. She isn't in Hell, hasn't replied to any of my messages magical or electrical. Alex would never avoid me purposely. I study the van, its windshield is broken, the engine is fried, a bloodbath in the back. Demons have different elements. There are fire, earth, air and water demons. Very few demons have all four, that right belongs to Alex, Lucifer, Alex's brother and his children. Flint is her brother's name and his sons are still growing into his powers but I'm sure they'll have their strengths. This one is an air demon. Only an air demon could take all these leaves off the trees, the fire to the engine was made to confuse me. It would have been more convincing if there wasn't a crushed lighter by the bonnet. Demons, I sigh. The bodies aren't there. The demon has moved them somewhere else. The demon has taken away our trail, masking scents in the wind. I need to return home and search my library for anything useful. My phone buzzes, 'location chip activated'. I smile, I gave Colt a chip to put on Abby. Demons aren't up with technology and she will never expect it.

Hell's Daughter

In my bedroom, all books relating to demons fly from the shelves. All demons have names, personalities and looks but only the important ones are documented. I pull out a book on air demons. I need to find out which demon and why. First, to find a list of demons who have a reason to be here. I record all the demons who are known for mass killings in their past history. That is most of them. There are a few known for their unusual evil doings.

I reach a list of ten in half an hour. I snap my fingers, a list of everyone who's been killed on my desk, pictures and a few facts on each. Records pulled from information during their lifetimes all found on the internet. The stack of twenty-four is appalling. It's only been two days and there has been twenty-four deaths in one area. The cops will be on a rapid search. There aren't any bodies so it'll all been missing person's cases, and it'll take a few days to realise how many are missing. I have already used my magic to hide any damage from the human eye. I deleted any footage of Abby because they will go after her, not the demon. Some of the ones who are murdered aren't human. So far it has been six women, six men and six children. They are all human. Then there have been six mortal supernaturals deaths too.

My heart plummets. No. I check, counting them all again. There are six of each. The devil's number. They aren't killing for fun, it's a ritual. The ritual is to bring Lucifer back to Earth by freeing him from my magic. That would explain going after Abby. It also means there are still six immortal supernaturals and six faerie folk left to kill.

"Shit!" I throw the pages in the air, they fall haphazardly around me. The demon in Abby is Silven, no doubt about it. She is the most powerful air demon. Loyal to Lucifer. She wants to free him and help him rule Hell. Silven should have no trouble controlling Abby constantly but she can't. I need to find out why. Maybe that can help me banish her for good. Or I'm going to

Hell's Daughter

have to kill Abby. For good. I don't want to do that to Colt, but if there is no way to extract the demon Abby will already be gone.

I slam the book onto the table in anger. Suffering the loss of an important person in your life is inevitable when you are immortal. My job is to prevent that happening to Colt for as long as possible. If there is a way to save Abby, I'll take it. Colt may have only been dating Abby for a few days, but he gets attached quickly.

"Are you okay?" Abby steps in my room.

"Yes." I grab the papers from the floor.

"Are you sure? I heard you curse."

"Yes. I just really need to contact Alex."

"Ah, you miss her already." Abby winks.

I try for a smile if only that was true. I don't want to kill Abby. Colt would hate me forever. And we have forever for him to hate me. I'd hate myself too, it is my fault Silven is after her in the first place.

"Come on, I can tell you like her. Ask her out."

I roll my eyes. "You don't know Alex, do you?" I ask sarcastically.

"I saw you two, she likes you. She may be the Queen of Hell, but I can tell."

I sigh, shaking my head. "Is it time for training?"

"Yes, come on." Abby skips out of my room.

I clench a fist.

I take a stick, the staff of bamboo in my hand. I grasp it tightly, Holly before me. Colt battles Abby.

"Try hit me." I offer.

Holly goes for the classic jab approach. Easy to counter. I block, sweeping my staff under her feet. A satisfying smack as her back hits the grass. Holly jumps to her feet going for an attack. The staff aims for my head. I yawn, lifting the staff with no effort. I push against her strength, sending her flat on her ass. Strength is useless if you don't have control and Holly has none.

"Come on, you can do better than that. I know you can." I demand.

Holly frowns. "You should loosen up a bit. I know you can." Holly retorts.

I raise an eyebrow. I can't say I was expecting the comeback. "I'm here to teach you, not the other way around."

Holly comes in, jumping forward. I sidestep and she topples on her chin. I offer my hand, she lies helplessly on the ground. Instantly, her staff catches between my feet, I land next to her. Well, I wasn't expecting that either. Yet, she is clumsy in her triumph. I stick my foot out and whack her around the back of the head with my staff when she tries to stand. She tumbles five times harder. Waiting, I circle her fallen body at a safe distance. I'm not stupid. I attack the second she gathers to her feet. Uncertain, she stands there like a sour lemon. My strike sends her reeling onto a tree before she can react.

"Think less." I teach.

"Less?" Holly's nose pinches.

"Yes, you like to read, don't you? Tell me about a book you are reading."

Holly frowns, waiting for a trick. I nod, encouraging her. I don't have all day.

"Okay, I'm reading a book called 'Midnight Rider' it's all about..."

I strike, she blocks it without thinking. Good.

"Then she finds this horse in a field." Thoughtlessly Holly makes a move of her own. I block it easily.

Holly continues to rattle on about the book, I don't listen. I zone out, till her mouth is simply moving making no sound. It must be one of the worst ever written. I don't understand romantic books, a few centuries back I was asked to write one. That didn't work out. A yelp catches me off guard from our casual duel. My head snaps to the noise by instinct. Colt, his back against a tree. Abby's staff at his neck. Abby had been struggling to get a shot in all morning. Colt's natural speed, strength and talent have seen to that. Currently, Colt is struggling under her strength and scrambling to push it off. Abby removes it begrudgingly.

"I have to go." Abby drops the staff.

"Where?" Colt asks.

"Home. I forgot something."

"I can magic it for you." I test.

"No." Her eyes light up to the sight of me. Shit. Abby's eyes glimmer unnaturally. This is a demon…

Silven

Waking, I hold a fragile bamboo stick in my hand. A young boy attacks, the same boy on my roof last night. I laugh, pathetic child. In a few seconds, his back is against the tree. His vampire nonsense is nothing in comparison to me. The boy is cute, for a vampire. I can smell it on him. My eyes flick to the onlookers. The twin and Enzo. How I wish to wrap my hands around his throat, watch him struggle in my grip as he dies. That would happen after much torture. I sigh in pleasure, the thought of his death is something I dream of often.

He thinks Alex will save him, protect him from harm simply because she is smitten with him. I bet she hasn't been responding to him recently. Once word spreads about my triumphant escape, they'll all come to their senses and join Lucifer and me in the rebellion. I'm counting on it. Currently, Alex will be wracking her brains for ideas of how to keep Hell at bay. She will not get a solution. I will kill Enzo for trapping Lucifer in Hell, our rightful ruler should not be treated so wrongly. I will have him soon. This boy will die. I'll make Enzo watch. Slowly, so he can feel every second of it. It's a known fact that the infamous Enzo has a horrific backstory, I've never known one worse. Losing this child will break him.

"I have to go!" I announce.

I need more bodies to release my dear Lucifer.

"Where?" The annoying brat of a boy asks.

"Home, I forgot something." I snap.

"I can magic it for you," Enzo suggests.

I scowl in his direction, yes just remind us all you are from Earth and Hell and incredibly unique. Being a Warlock and a Hellhound gives him the power to trap Lucifer in Hell. Luckily, the reversal of such a spell requires him to die. The spell is connected to him, to break it, you must break the binder. It is in the ritual.

"No." I storm off, I have no more time for this tea party. I have people to kill. The daylight streams on my horrible human skin. I sigh, humans are more alert to criminal activity during the daylight. I'll have to prepare for now. I walk in the direction of my lair, ears listening for anyone who dares follow. None of the group follows their dear friend. Good.

Reaching my humble lair, I climb into the cave. The pile of bodies sits there. The spell to remove such a curse sits on a wall along with the ingredients, ashes from Hell, candles and the symbol in which the bodies must be placed. The special space for Enzo in the middle. In a ring of glorious fire. After he recites the reversing spell all the bodies will go up in flames. Lucifer will come back from Hell and rise again. I need followers, in case of complications. I pull out parchment paper, writing a letter to all the demons who wish to live in Lucifer's reign again. There are many to recruit.

Hell's Daughter

Enzo

Watching Silven go I don't try and stop her. Silven won't know modern technology and won't find the chip. We'll follow her once she stops moving. She can't kill anyone in broad daylight. Colt meets my eye. I nod.

"Abby!" Holly calls jogging the way Silven had gone.

"Stop!" I demand.

"Why?"

Frustrated, I pull out my phone. Pulling up the navigation app it shows her location. Good.

"Why can't we follow Abby?" Holly frowns.

I glance at Colt, I don't want to explain. Colt can give her the information sympathetically. I cannot.

"Sit down, we need to tell you something."

Colt sits Holly down supportively. Holly is not going to take this well.

"What is it?" Holly worries rightfully.

"Basically, demons can inhabit bodies…"

"Abby's been possessed!" Holly squawks, she catches on quickly.

"Yes, we need to follow her."

"When? How? Why?"

"It started…"

"No time." I wave my phone. "We have to go, we can portal there."

Silven isn't that far away, she is still in the forest.

"Is she still in there?" Holly asks.

I watch the phone. I can spare the time, we didn't have to leave that soon, but I wanted to avoid that conversation.

"Normally, no but somehow Abby seems to be getting brief hours of control. We are still trying to find out why."

"Can we help her?" Holly asks, worry clouding her face.

"Yes. We will try." The dot on the map is moving. "We have to go."

"Go?" Holly looks astonished.

"Yes. We have to stop the demon, her name is Silven."

I wave my hand. Weapons appear in their hands. A dagger in hers and dual blades for Colt, I taught him with those daggers.

"I'm not fighting my sister."

"You aren't. It's Silven and she is killing a lot of people."

"How do you know? How long have you known?"

"A few days. Come on." I whisk up a portal.

"Why didn't you tell me!" Holly protests, eyes blazing in fury. "Does Abby know?"

"She doesn't and it seemed unnecessary to tell you till now," I reply waving for her to go through the damn portal.

"No! You should have told me. I'm her sister!" Holly snaps.

I roll my eyes, her problems aren't really important at the moment. Stopping Silven is. Especially knowing that she wants to bring back Lucifer. The spell won't be fun for any of us. Casually, I push Holly's whiney ass through the portal.

"Enzo!" Colt watches as she screams, tumbling inside.

I grin. "Oops." I won't lie and say that didn't feel good. "Let's go."

Slipping through the portal, I have taken us to a spot Silven won't see us. My ears prick up.

"Can you hear that?" Holly asks, her ears perking up.

"Yes." The scratching noise rattles my ears, the noise of a nail on a cave wall. Through the thick trees, I see a dim cave entrance.

"Holly, you need to transform," I order.

"Why?"

"To attack." What else would it be?

"I'm not fighting my sister." She point blank refuses. "I don't care what you say."

"She is not your sister anymore." I try to persuade her, it's for her own protection. "Colt back me up here. We won't be hurting Abby because it isn't her anymore."

"We need to get the demon while hurting Abby as little as possible." Colt doesn't take my side but he doesn't go against me either.

I sigh. "I didn't say we should kill her, just chain her up which might require an attack."

"No!" Holly snaps angrily, I hear a bone pop. At this rate, she'll be attacking me.

"That is Silven, she is a demon. She won't hesitate to harm us."

"Abby is in there! You don't hurt the people you love!" Holly's irritating voice continues. "I bet you have never loved anyone! Ever! That is why you don't give a shit. You don't care, do you?"

I scowl. My fists clench. If I didn't give a shit, why am I here? Holly is bold to make such accusations.

"You have no idea about my life. So, shut up and help us or I'll portal you back."

"I'm not going anywhere. I'm not letting you hurt my sister."

Holly wields the knife in my direction. She is picking the wrong side. She would never get a shot in. The only chance I have is to show her that it is not her sister.

CHAPTER ELEVEN

Silven

My ears perk up to the glorious song of an argument. I grin cheerily when I realise who it is. The infamous Enzo. By tomorrow night, he'll be dead and Lucifer will be ruling Hell and Earth. I will be alongside him like I've always been. Alex will not stop us again. She'll be easy to kill after Enzo is gone. She'll come running to mourn him. I heard the whispers in the echoing cells, Alex is soft on the boy. My body surges with the energy of the demons who have joined me in our rebellion. News spreads quickly in Hell, the fact I have escaped has brought back hope to the demons that Lucifer can return. The idea that Alex is not as powerful as she makes herself out to be entering the demons' minds, and together we can beat her. Most demons cannot resurface until Lucifer is free, but I can feel their strength behind me. The plan is engraved in my mind, after all those years thinking of it, it is finally coming to life.

Picking up one of the bodies I carve the human symbol in its fragile chest. My lips quirk a smile, the bird symbol, normally birds represent freedom and beauty. These humans are neither.

Hell's Daughter

Each body must bear the mark to be used in the ceremony. It connects all of them so they become one. There is something about a dead body that causes a twinge of joy runs through my body. The mound of corpses is a great achievement in my life. I have killed many more, the plagues have been thrilling. Bringing back Lucifer will be my greatest accomplishment ever.

A shadow looms at the edge of my cave. The werewolf girl hasn't been taught how to blend into her surroundings yet. She is the weakest link. The link I can use to play out my plan. Wiping my bloody hands on a random jacket worn by one of the dead, I pick up the knife. Chains whip in my direction. I laugh, child's play, a wave of the hand and they switch direction. Enzo, mightiest of them all, forces the chains to disappear before they hit him. What a shame. The three musketeers block the only exit.

"Children." I hiss, lips curling.

"Abby?" The girl steps forward, breaking their formation.

I hear Enzo, wizard of wizards, sigh. I tuck a small object away on my person. I step forward into the light, revealing the face the twin knows and loves.

"Yes." I don't remember the silly werewolf's name. "I- I need your help."

That's it, the werewolf skids my way. Sailing, arms wrapping around my neck. I laugh at the comedy. I grab her neck, slamming her head into the wall. A squeal.

"Is that all it took to convince you?" I chuckle.

The vampire hurtles my way. Snapping my fingers, a gust of wind sends him into a wall. Where did Enzo get these people? They are useless. The twin struggles in my grip, in a daze.

"Move, I will kill her." The knife digs in her throat.

Colt, the vampire boy freezes. As if a simple waggle of his bony finger would get her killed, it's Enzo's fingers I need to watch. Enzo paces forward, I push the knife in further. Struggling, the werewolf girl fights helplessly. "Foolish girl." My mouth drools with venom. "Love will kill you."

"Abby, come back to me, please. I know you are in there. Please, for me. I want to be there for you. Fight her! Please!" The daft girl begs.

I roll my eyes. That won't work. I let the knife slice into her throat just a little. Enzo, son of a bitch, waves a magical hand at me. My knife goes right for the kill. The blade glides out of my fingertips before I can make the cut. I snarl, two can play at this game. Wind billowing around me, rocks pour from the ceiling. In a whirlwind, they circle my body. Sharp spikes in the rocks, enough to kill a person.

"Get down!" Enzo calls out to the scared children.

My rocks blast out, in all directions striking for their bodies.

"Holly. Move." Colt ducks for her.

Holly, that is her name. Blasting through the cave, razor-sharp rocks enter the vampire's skin. Rolling to his side, he gasps, the rocks sticking out from his body, all on his left side. Enzo ducks to safety, to my disappointment.

"No!" Holly screams.

Enzo, the bastard, sends a wave of magic in my direction. I block it. Enzo rolls forward and sends another wave. I chuckle, blocking it again. Even with enhanced powers, he can't get a shot in. My victory is short-lived, I understand why Enzo went forward. Enzo grabs one of my wrists, flipping my small fragile human body over his shoulder. I hear a crack. Pain jolts down my back. I forgot how delicate the human body is. Scrambling to my feet, I wrap a hand around his throat. He draws a knife out his sleeve.

"No!"

Something plucks at my brain, not a knife but more of a mental pain. My hand falls limp. The girl is taking back her body. By the devil! I need more time. It's a good thing I've planned for this. Kicking Enzo square in the stomach, he rolls away. Rocks, one after the other penetrate him, magic flies from his fingertips. He blocks each approach before flipping over my head. Not unexpectedly, Enzo loves his magic tricks. Spinning, I

Hell's Daughter

grab a knife from his sleeve as he goes over. Slashing, it cuts his neck and skims his ear. Enzo, the material arts idiot, kicks me in my head. I fall in the dirt. Pain comes over my body. Humans are too weak for their own good. Blood, ink-black pours from my wound.

"Abby! Stop this now!" Holly screams, the werewolf lives up to her name, eyes glowing a faint yellow colour. She'll regret this move. In her last few seconds to live, my foot staggers. My hand stops mid-motion with the knife. No. Abby is fighting me. I fly across the small cave, using my precious time left. My knife goes right for her heart, I need to shut Holly up. Abby will have less of a reason to fight with her twin dead. Holly's scream rings out... A voice in my head stronger, yelling louder.

Abby

I pounce, knife in the air. I head right for Holly who is screaming. No! Mid-air inches from Holly. I can't stop the knife, it'll hit her. I can't move it out the way. I can't drop it either, it'll land on her. Shaking, I point the blade away from her, the flat base going in her direction. Landing on top of Holly, I wheeze. I stab myself in the side as a consequence. Pain, my side rips open. I wheeze, the knife tickles my insides with each touch of the handle. Not again. My head is spinning in the dark surroundings.

"Abby?" Holly grabs me, putting me in her lap for support. What is going on? I hiss, the blade in the area of my intestines. Lifeblood drains from the wound. Groaning, I can feel the pain spreading in my body.

Swivelling my head to find Enzo and Colt, I see we are in a cave, dark wet ground under my body. Propping myself up, my side throbbing harder. I notice them, Enzo bends over Colt who has half a dozen rocks sticking out his body. I can't see any further in the dark cave. My heart pounds. There is no-one else here. Colt groans, removing the rocks one by one. A fist-sized stone from his rib cage becomes loose. The knife trembles, I still clutching the handle. Did I do this?

"Heal her," Holly begs.

I look at my side, the wound doesn't look fatal.

"Is it her?" Enzo glares in my direction. "Do you remember when we went to the beach?"

"We never went to the beach." Why does everyone keep asking if I remember events?

"Good. It's her." Enzo kneels beside me, fixing up my wound.

Who else would it be? "What happened?"

"You are possessed by a demon. Silven. She wants to bring Lucifer back from Hell." Enzo states bluntly.

My eyes widen, I don't hear him right. "What?"

Colt glares at Enzo. "Demons can take control of a human body. The one inside you is called Silven. Normally, you would be lost in your body forever but somehow you take back control."

I did hear right. A demon, a miserable beast from the underworld is in my body.

"So, we don't have to kill you." Enzo lets go of my shirt. All the pain releases from my side.

"What? Kill me?" I ask, stunned. I know Enzo isn't fond of me, but I didn't realise he has been planning to kill me.

"You normally can't save someone from possession. We are going to try." Colt promises.

My heart thuds. Enzo grabs a piece of paper from the wall. Slowly, it begins to burn to ash.

"Let's go."

I have no more time for questions, I stagger into the portal with the others in a blur.

Landing in Enzo's living room we sit on the sofa. My heart pounds, I don't say a word. There is a demon inside of me.

Hell's Daughter

Momentarily, I close my eyes to calm down. It'll be fine, for now. Colt forces Enzo to magic up hot chocolate. I take a sip, it's the best hot chocolate I've ever tasted. I curl up in the corner seat.

"If a demon possesses me, how do I get rid of it?"

They said I was fighting it, surely there is a way for me to purge it from my body.

"We must track it from the beginning. To find out what makes you able to fight for your own consciousness."

I nod. Enzo kicks back his feet in his dedicated chair. It has books neatly on the table beside it, no empty mugs, the chair rocks slightly, old-style wood, carved neatly. Obviously, it is his chair, I bet Colt has never sat on it.

"It started after Callum attacked us." I input, starting the conversation.

"Which means it happened during the attack. Probably while you were dead. It would be easier to take control." Enzo puts in.

"Dead?" Holly howls in shock.

Enzo's lips go into a thin line, grimacing. Holly and he aren't friends yet it seems. Colt seems equally surprised. "What? You were dead?"

"You are correct, she was. Alex's blood can bring people back to life. Let's move on." Enzo hurries on the conversation.

"Do you think that is why I have control some of the time?"

"The blood heals and revives the body. I've never heard of it being able to purge demons."

"Is that a no?"

"It's a possibility. It is not something I would try unless we were desperate."

I shiver, Colt wraps an arm around my shoulder, I can feel he is tense. He isn't comfortable sitting with me, worrying if I will try and throttle him any second. Even Holly sat on another sofa. Enzo doesn't look afraid, he is thinking logically. He touches a horn gently, I forgot all about them. Before, it was the first thing I noticed. Slowly, I take another sip of the creamy hot chocolate.

"Even so, it is wearing off, Silven is coming more and more frequently."

"Do you mean Silven might take control completely?"

My heart pounds. I might lose myself forever. I don't want that. I would die, and there would be no way to save me. I would be gone, with a demon walking around wearing my face. I would be dead, in a deep sleep with no hope. It could happen any second and I have no way to stop it. I take a deep breath. I can't focus on that unless I want to have a panic attack. I must focus on how to stop it. I can't think of anything other than the blood that seems to have had a chance of helping me fight the demon. That is the only unusual event that happened to me. But even if that is true, it is wearing away and not a permanent fix.

"We need a long-term solution." Colt tears through the silence. "How do we get rid of demon possession? There must be a way."

Enzo shrugs. "I'm not sure, it is likely it has been done before but if it were easy people wouldn't resort to killing the possessed."

"Great." I murmur. Enzo doesn't help my enthusiasm.

Silven

Snapping alive, I'm in Enzo's living room. I am gaining more and more control, good.

My eyes glimpse out the window, it can't have been more than an hour, the sun is still up. I can feel her measly efforts to take over, a tickle in the back of my brain. I have incorporated this inconvenient child into my plan. Luckily for her, she'll get to return once more before I don't let her back, leaving her stuck in a small space in her mind. There is just one thing I need to do first.

Hell's Daughter

I check my shoe, it is still there for my next awakening. I jump from Colt's embrace. I don't understand human intimacy. I walk off to the doorway. There is a backdoor in the kitchen. I can see it. Striding forward, Enzo blocks the entrance in a flash.

"Where are you going?" He asks bluntly.

"The kitchen, I want to wash off the blood."

I point to my hands, a few flecks of blood on each. Enzo moves out my way, his eyes fixate on my back. I can sense it. The sink is a few metres from the door. It'll be locked. I start the tap and bolt. Grabbing the door, shaking it. A blast of severe energy connects with my spine. My eyes water, the pain unbearable. That is more power than a warlock should have, especially a hybrid. In agony, I collapse. I let go of control of the body. Abby can deal with it now, I've done what I had to do.

Abby

I collapse, an intense electric pulse stops my body moving. Spasming on the floor, my head spins. Howling, I cry out, the immense pain too much to bear. Tears flood down my cheeks. My body feels like it's on fire. Jolting all over the floor, I have no control over my body. Vomit churning, I throw up all over myself. My sight fades to the flashing lights. Distant voices echo in my head. Unable to stay awake any more, I drift off.

I gasp, I am on the kitchen floor. How did I get here?

"What have you done Enzo?" Colt kneels by my body.

I twinge a finger. "Hello?" I croak. "Colt?"

"Abby?"

I nod. "Party. Kiss." The two words I can manage to confirm it is me.

"What did you do to her Enzo?"

"Paralyse her." Enzo flicks a hand in my direction.

Subsiding the pain releases from my body. I wheeze for breath. My shirt is covered in my vomit. Enzo did that to me? I would prefer knife wounds over that. Magic puts me in new clean clothes, the stench of vomit gone.

"Abby are you okay?" Colt helps me to my feet.

My legs shake slightly. "Yeah— I think so. Did she take control again?"

"Yeah for two minutes."

I shudder, Enzo is powerful. The pain from the blast was worse than dying. I guess that was the point. It was directed at Silven, not me. Walking back to the sofa, I flop into the cushions.

Enzo disappears and reappears like a ghost, holding twenty-plus books in his hands, they pile over his face. More trail behind him.

"Why don't you just carry all of them with magic?"

"I'm not that lazy," Enzo answers bluntly, letting go of the books, a table appears under them before they fall. Handcuffs drop into Enzo's hand swinging there. "May I suggest we use these?"

"You want to cuff me?" I ask.

"Yes. To one of us preferably."

I agree. He has a point. It will stop Silven running away like she did. I take it and it clicks around my wrist, then Colt takes the other half. I would pick Holly, but she would fall for Silven's tricks and she doesn't have the skills to defend herself. I don't think Enzo would want to be cuffed to me. Colt is my best hope, he won't fall for Silven's tricks and is not as aggressive as Enzo. If there was hope, he wouldn't try and kill me.

There is a chance that there will be no hope left at some point. I will not return. Enzo seems willing to kill me if that happens. Not that I would blame him, I would want him to, if it came to it. I wouldn't want anyone to die because of me. If Silven truly takes over my body, I'm already gone. Colt has the skills, but he wouldn't kill me. Holly wouldn't either. I pull out my phone. I appreciate why Colt and Holly wouldn't kill me but I need a security blanket.

I text Enzo. 'Will you kill me. If it comes to it?'

Enzo takes his nose out of his book and checks it. An answer bleeps back. 'Is that what you want?'

I take a deep breath. 'Yes'

'Then done.'

I stick my phone on the sideboard before the other two get suspicious.

"Start reading." Enzo hands out the books.

I pick mine 'Stories of demonic possession and how to detect it'. I flip open to a page I wish I hadn't. Demons are all over the page, they look terrifying. Worse than anyone has imagined them to be, all the books and movies are hardly accurate. Scanning the page, it starts and finishes with death. I flip from story to story. They are identical, death and destruction every time.

Yawning, I put down the second book. My hot chocolate doesn't run out, whenever it sinks it replaces immediately. Colt has fallen asleep on my shoulder. Enzo doesn't seem to notice anything pages fly by, how can he even read that quickly. Holly is in her natural element, hunching over a book in intense concentration. It reminds me of when we revised for our SAT's together. She would whiz through the textbooks, get each answer right when we quizzed one another. She is highly intelligent and soaks in every drop of information and embeds it in her brain. I smile. I hope I don't have to let go of all of this. I really don't. It's not my life I'm scared of losing. It's getting to see my family, hanging out with friends and not being there for them. I haven't seen Kyle in days. A tear slips down my cheek, I never asked what Silven has done while trying to bring back Lucifer. I don't want to know. I try not to think about it. My eyes droop sleepily, I shake my head, wipe away the tears and sip the hot chocolate.

CHAPTER TWELVE

Silven

I'm back! At my own free will. The girl will not be returning this time. The night sky glimmers through the glass ceiling. Colt sleeps beside me. I pull away from Colt, what is wrong with this girl? My hand gets caught, I look back to find a chain. Of course. I bet it was Enzo, Lord of Bastards', idea. I should have expected as much. They think I'm going to run, my plan is working. My plot to take him is a whole lot easier. Enzo, top on my most wanted list, skim reads a book. Holly reading at a human pace. Both none the wiser of my return.

Slowly, I examine the room for a weapon, there are mugs and plates all over the tables. They will do. I want something empty. There is a mug, I lean and peer inside, trying not to tug on the chain. It's full, doesn't this girl drink? I take a sip of the foul liquid, almost choking. Why do human's drink such concoctions? I put it back down. The rest of the food looks equally unappetising. The only human food I enjoy is cheese. It works well with all demon food. I don't understand why humans eat it with other foods. Ruins it. I look back down into the cup, it's full again. Stupid Enzo. It doesn't matter, I will simply have to make a larger mess. I fumble the cup, dropping it onto the floor. Shattering to pieces, the mug breaks.

"Oh no! I'm so sorry." I try not to let the words drip sarcastically.

Enzo looks up from his book. I yank on the chain a little, trying to scoop up the shards.

"Let me clean it up." Holly jumps in to help. I pick up the largest shard and stab it into her arm.

"Abby!" She squeals, clutching her forearm.

I aim again for her chest.

"Enough!" Enzo's hands of unfortunate magic rise. Grabbing Colt, I pull him close, wrap my hands around his throat. He jolts awake.

"No-one move!"

I reveal the broken shard in my hands. One wrong move and I slit his throat. How beautiful that would be. Holly trembles on the floor, she isn't going to move. Enzo look at Colt with fear in his eyes. I smile, I caused that. Fear in the almighty Enzo, it is one of the most beautiful sights I have ever seen. I most look forward to his death.

"Let him go," Enzo argues.

"No. He's my way of getting what I want."

Enzo's lips tighten, the bastard. "Let him go and you can have what you want."

"That won't work, we both know that." I hiss.

I want Enzo. I need him to recite the spell but if they were to swap places, Enzo would blast himself free as soon as we were out of harm's way. Then he would send me back to Hell and kill the girl I possess. The trade has to be later, when I am prepared.

"Meet me at my home in twenty-four hours from now. No sooner, no later or he dies."

I waggle my shoe, the wires of a bomb slide out into view. "I'm going to arm this on dear Colt. If you go near him in the next twenty-four hours, it'll explode killing both of you. But stick to my rules and I'll disarm it and release him."

Hell's Daughter

Enzo, king of dumb-asses, nods. "Fine."

Colt jumps, I laugh as the shard digs into his throat. Choking, the boy gasps. Did he honestly think that would work?

"See you soon."

I wink, and a gust of wind sends us flying out the window into the night sky. Colt dangling by the chain, howling.

Enzo

"Shit. Shit. Shit!" I yell in anger, china sailing across the room. I flip a table. "Fuck!"

I chuck a chair across the room. It smashes to pieces.

"Enzo. Enzo please calm down." Holly orders.

I run my hands through my hair, eyes wide. We are in deep shit. Silven has Colt. I will not let Colt die. Never. How could I have let this happen? I shouldn't have let them be handcuffed to each other. It should have been me. Damn it! Lock Lucifer in Hell. Sure, why not? He's a bastard, the world will be a better place without him. Alex is more powerful, a better leader and cares about humans. But where the fuck is she? She should be trying to stop this monstrosity of a situation. I haven't even got a text back.

"Enzo!" Holly's voice screams above my thoughts.

"What?" I howl back.

"Calm down!" Holly begs.

I take a deep breath. Alex will be here. I know that she is late, but she'll come eventually. I hope. Closing my eyes, I take a second before opening them again. I stare in a mirror, smashed to pieces. I see my face, horns and orange eyes. I turn to my living room. Fire. The entire room is ablaze. My furniture, books, the old crystal chandelier drops, smashing to pieces. My body blazes in the fires of Hell that run throughs my veins. Holly stamps desperately on the flames that are consuming the house. Smoke clouds the building. The fire is already spreading throughout the house. Shit. Squeezing my hands shut, the flames flicker, shrinking and diminishing. In a minute, the fire is out. The wallpaper is burnt away, the bricks holding up. I haven't lost control in centuries.

Holly sways, coughing hard. "Thank-god. I thought you were going to burn your house to ashes."

"We need a plan. Come with me. We don't have much time."

"Where are we going?"

"To my second home." I grab a box from the top shelf, a small wooden box of Alex's blood. I whisk up a portal.

"Second home? You live in a mansion, why do you have two?"

"I have multiple homes, we are going to my safe house."

Holly jumps through, I follow. I'll fix it. No matter what. I swear.

In my apartment, I open the dusty blinds. The apartment is bland and almost empty. Two cushions on the living room floor, a bathroom and another room with two single beds with no sheets. There is food on shelves with large bottles of water.

"Is this a bunker?" Holly stares in awe.

"Yes, of a kind."

"What do we do now? My sister and Colt are with the crazy demon." She asks.

"Find a way to save them." I put down the box.

"Is that the death cure?" Holly strokes the polish wooden lid.

"Yes."

"Why not let Colt die and bring him back after?"

I shake my head, that wouldn't work.

"That will not stop her. She won't stop trying to get what she wants. We need a plan to get rid of her for good." I snap my fingers, books on demon possession's cures appear. There aren't many. I doubt they will have answers. Lounging on the cushions, I pick up a book.

Five hours later, Holly squeals. "Found one!"

I grab the book quickly. It's a cure. We need a special sword. I curse. The Sword of Angels.

"What?" Holly can't breathe in suspense.

My hope diminishes.

"The Sword of Angels. The one we need. It was destroyed over one hundred years ago. An angel could make one with their blood but we can't contact them. Even so, they are stubborn bastards they wouldn't help us."

Tears flush Holly's cheeks, pouring silently. She had hope, more than I did. It's her sister after all. Grabbing my arm, she hugs me, crying without making a peep. I can hear her heartbeat drumming manically in her chest in fear. The silent cries are the most painful. I squeeze her arm back. We may not have the Sword of Angels but we have more knowledge that can help.

"We are going to get Abby back, I promise."

Holly jumps to her feet, rage over her entire face.

"How? One way. One. That was all we had and the blasting sword was destroyed. My sister is gone. A demon controls her. I can't help her. No-one can!" Holly rages. "You can't promise me anything. Nothing. You keep your stupid mouth shut. You can still save Colt with that stupid blood. I can't save my sister. It is all your fucking fault too! You are the one who helped Alex, you are the one who Silven wants. It's you!"

That is why I never wanted to help Holly in the first place. Many people have died because they knew me. I took on Colt, I had to. I made a promise. I stopped doing small jobs for Alex after I took him in. I thought that would protect him. But the past never fails to sneak up on me. That is why I refuse to allow Colt or Abby to die.

"We can save Abby." I need her to hear me out.

"Don't you dare say that unless you mean it!"

Holly's face is red in rage, bones clicking. I can see her trying to fight the transformation.

"I have a plan A," I answer.

"Plan A?" Holly stops, bones clicking back in place. "You thought of something?"

"Listen."

"That is an excellent plan and yet terrible," Holly says once I finish. "No, we can't do that."

"Unless you have another plan A, we have to do this," I argue. "You want Abby back, I want Colt to be safe. I don't like you having so much responsibility either but…"

Holly cuts me off. "That is not what I am talking about."

I sigh. "It'll be okay."

I pour all the samples of blood in a larger potion glass. I do up the lid and hand it over to Holly.

"Force it down Silven's throat. All of it. Don't miss a drop." I order.

An angel's blood is used in the sword. We have half-angel blood. Abby was right, it was the blood.

"One can help Abby fight it, nine doses can purge Silven from her body for good."

"That's easier said than done."

Carefully, Holly pockets it, the tube bulging in her pocket. I wave a hand, the bulge disappears. It has a protection spell to stop it from shattering.

"Do you have to complete the spell?" Holly asks.

"Yes. Once I start it is impossible to stop. That's why you are to cure Abby before Silven finishes.

"How does she finish the ritual?"

"Pouring her blood into the circle and drawing the symbol of freedom.

"Okay. I can stop that." Holly nods.

"Good because I won't be there to help."

"Are you sure you want to do this? I mean you'll have no memories. You said it'll fry your brain."

"Better than dying." I smile.

Hell's Daughter

Holly doesn't laugh, but nods. From under the floorboards, I pull up a weapon stash.

"Wow, it's like a minefield down here." Holly touches the weapons gently.

"Take what you can use."

"You have a gun?"

Holly picks it up. A ring, I duck as a shot is fired. My ear bleeds where it had skimmed me. The bullet sits in the wall behind me.

"You idiot!" I yell. "You cannot have a gun."

Holly is halfway across the room, running from the gun she fired. I scoop it up and carefully put it away out of reach.

"Why aren't you taking weapons?"

"I don't need them. None of them are for me, I use claws or magic."

She clutches a blade, with terrible form.

"Here, I'll teach you to use it."

"Thanks." Holly smiles. "You are a good person, I'm sorry for everything I've said."

"Don't worry about it." I hold her hands, "You place it like this to…"

Silven

In the cave, I whisk the handcuff off of my wrist and it goes around Colt's. I stick his hands behind his back. Ordinary cuffs would be easy for the vampire to break, but Enzo supplied this pair. They were designed to hold me. Colt is not breaking out of them. I chuck him in the corner. I chain up his feet, I'd found the chain in the back of my van, it's thick and heavy. He'll struggle to break it if it's even possible . I apply the bomb to his chest. I stole it on one of my nights out. It's very nice, I have the detonator.

"Be a good boy when I'm gone," I smirk.

Sailing off into the night sky, I have more bodies to collect to complete my sacrifice. They will not be hard to find. I can sense a supernatural from a mile away. I catch wind of a pixie. They blend in well with humans. Their pointy ears and wide eyes are the most noticeable features. The pixie is in her car on her way home from work. Landing on her car, she screams her voice high pitch. Another sign of a pixie. I lean over the windshield, smashing it. She steers the car, we go off into a lamppost. I grab her by the shirt. She throws a punch. I block, with a sigh. Pointy teeth appear out her mouth. Snarling she lunges to bite in my neck. I wrench her hair, sending her head in the steering wheel. Again, and again. Blood and brain splatters in the broken glass. Another down... few more to go.

Returning, Colt yells and yanks on his chains uselessly. I bet he did it the entire time I was gone. I have collected my bodies. I start to arrange them in their rings going outwards. First children, then women, men, mortal supernaturals, immortal supernaturals then six faerie folk. I lay salt on the ground. I hum a demon tune while I work to block out the noise of the whining child in my cave. Tonight will be fun, no doubt about it. I chuckle to myself. I will finally see dear Enzo, on his knees. Then dead as the soil in Hell.

I grab Colt by the back of his shirt while he thrashes about in my grasp. It is time. The day has gone quickly, I have been waiting enthusiastically for Enzo at the entrance of my cave. I pull the struggling vampire to the ritual site for the exchange. I have untied his feet so he can walk.

"Abby? Now would be a really good time to wake up." The boy pulls against my grip.

I wave the detonator. "Your girl isn't coming back."

Colt stops fighting, his eyes fall on the ritual. Bodies in their ring, their symbols engraved into their chests, a few corpses have been eaten away by worms in the cave. I tried to preserve them for as long as possible. Their state will not affect the ritual, the ritual just requires that they were all killed in a ten-day period. The clock strikes, it is time for their arrival.

On cue, Enzo and Holly appear before me. Holly goes sickly pale at the preparation for the ritual. Enzo doesn't bat an eye or pay any attention. He's left room between us and them in the teleport. Sensible choice.

"Wait there." I wave the detonator.

Enzo scowl is pure anger giving me goosebumps. I drink in that look. Knowing I'd see that look is all that kept me going in the cell.

"Get in the circle," I order. "Don't try anything."

Enzo storms over, trudging through all the bodies, I hear a hand break under his boot.

"Careful!" I call.

Enzo stands in the ring of hell ash and bodies I've prepared for him.

"Release Colt," Enzo growls.

"No. Start the ritual. Then I will." My mouth struggles with the words. "I promise."

"Your promises mean nothing to me." Enzo spits.

"Start or I blow him up."

"If you blow him up. I won't do it."

The smart ass. "Fine. I'll pass him to Holly as you start."

Enzo nods grimly. He knows there is no way to save Colt without doing it. My hand can move as fast on the button than his hands can with magic.

Holly shakes slightly next to me. I don't watch her, she is no threat. I listen to Enzo. A single word leaving his lips while I pass over the detonator. Holly crushes it, destroying the circuits. The bomb can no longer be activated. I don't bother, I watch Enzo. His mouth moves, waving to the earth intensely. Magic pours from his hands into the earth's ground. Lines soar along with the earth, weaving between the bodies and connecting in streaks of green and blue I see Enzo grimace visibly as his mouth opens. "Inveierte mi hechizo. Toma estos sacrificos para alimentar la tierra."

I drop Colt. He'll die soon anyway. Once Lucifer rises, joy floods in my veins. I did it! I actually did it.

CHAPTER THIRTEEN

Enzo

I create a portal for us to travel through. Holly grasps my hand and squeezes it for support. I can hear her heart rattling in her chest. I smile reassuringly. I step through. We walk through the second, we are meant to be there. We couldn't be a minute earlier or late. Silven would think the deal was off.

On the other side, I spot the horrific sight of all the people. Dead and prepared for the ritual. Symbols engraved in all their chests. What was I expecting? I don't bother giving her the satisfaction of a reaction. I walk towards them. Colt is struggling.

"Wait there." Silven waves to the destination.

My teeth clench together, my fingers itch to hit her with all the magic and fire in my veins. But that won't work. She grins, tauntingly. "Get in the circle."

Neither of us is stupid, I won't start without knowing Colt is safe. She won't blow him up before I start or I have no reason to help her. I trudge through the bodies, there is a special path for me, I don't take it. I charge through the bodies.

"Careful!" Silven yells as I break a dead woman's hand.

Trinity-Rose Crane

Hell's Daughter

I walk in the circle of ash in the centre. "Release Colt!" I growl.

We argue till she agrees to release him as I start. Holly is there ready to take him. She'll whisper the plan and take action. I channel the magic, beads of it flutter in the ground creating channels of energy. I watch Silven. I don't trust her but currently, I don't have a choice. My mouth opens to the words that will trap me in the ring until I finish.

"Inveierte mi hechizo. Toma estos sacrificos para alimentar la tierra."

The detonator cracks, Colt drops from her grasp.

My heart beats rapidly in my chest, my hands begin to shake. I draw a breath, the strong power of the spell floods through me. I stop talking, beads of sweat roll down my forehead. I need to continue. Heat flashes over me. The power of Hell pressures my body to utter the next words against my will. Agony pulses through my body.

Silven

Holly holds Colt. He's hungry. He hasn't had blood in over twenty-four hours.

"Go, kids, run while you still can. It won't be long till Lucifer rises." They still won't escape, but I would love a running target.

"Stop! Enzo! Stop!" Colt screams.

"He can't." Holly shakes her head.

She bends down to help him struggle to his feet. Vampire teeth emerge from his lips as he fights his hunger. A skill he learnt from his dying master. The two talk, I ignore the rodents. This moment will go down in history, the demons will always remember it.

"Go before I kill you myself."

To my surprise, Colt spins from his crouched position and a punch connects right with my face. I stumble.

"Foolish boy!"

Colt grabs my arm, drinking hungrily guzzling like a pack animal.

"Get off me!"

I scream, sending a whirlwind at him. He thwacks against a tree trunk. Blood soaks his clothes. My blood. More like Abby's. Demon blood is very potent. I guess they care less for Abby then they make out. Holly charges blades drawn, she can't use those. Child. I dodge with a simple sidestep.

I grab her wrist as she passes by and flip her on her back. "I told you not to do that."

Her face smiles brightly. Pain throbs in my stomach, blood pooling out my stomach. The knife she wields is stained in blood. She has impaled my skin twice while I flipped her. Enzo, smart maggot, taught her that trick. Feet kick my thigh, sending me kneeling against my will.

"Get her!" Colt yells, arms wrapping around me.

"No!" With all my power, howling wind shakes the trees, leaves flutter everywhere.

"You don't want to break your precious circle, do you?" Holly retorts.

I grit my teeth, she is right. The wind dies down. I'll just have to find another way to get rid of them. Colt's foot connects with my back. I wheeze at the crack. My back throbs. I gasp, trying to struggle to my feet a person flips me onto my front. A foot goes to my neck.

"I swear! You children! You don't want to kill your friend." The boot sinks in. I cough, choking as I try to tug him off. My eyes dart to my ritual site. My hand flickers. Colt flies through the air and smacks into a bush. I laugh. A small red bottle enters my mouth, spluttering. The liquid flows down my throat forcefully. The irony taste in my mouth.

"What did you do to me?" I snarl.

Hell's Daughter

"I did it!" The glass bottle drops from Holly's hand.

I grab her collar. "What did you do?"

"Save Abby from you, asshole." Colt stumbles, removing a branch from his shoulder.

"What? No. I'm so close." My fingers tremble.

Enzo

I watch them fight. More or less get their asses kicked. Silently praying they can do it. I relax a little as Holly pours the liquid down Silven's throat. I watch it drip down, every last drop. They did it. My mouth utters the spell I wish I didn't know. I knew they could do it. They will have Abby back and Silven won't finish the ritual. I still have to finish my part.

Flashing back, I sit arguing back with Holly discussing plan A. I remember hesitating whether, to tell the truth, or to lie. Holly would do anything to save her sister, nothing we had to do would change that. It's the one quality I truly like about her. I chose to lie to her, to make her consciousness less guilty. I told her I would lose my memories and it would fry my brain. The last part was almost true. The ritual is so draining it'll kill me, I have to be the last sacrifice to finish it. My mouth moves over the Spanish gracefully. The whispers of demons rattle my mind. I can hear them. Ready to come with Lucifer. To kill and destroy as they do. Sweat drips down my forehead, my hands shake with the will of the demons. This is it.

"Y ahora me sacrifico para liberar a Lucifer y traer el infierno a la tierra."

A flame blazes over all the bodies then fades. Gasping I can finally breathe. Tears roll down my cheeks from the pain. My eyes begin to flutter. Colt is standing over Abby, who will wake up any second, free from Silven. My eyes drift closed and begin to fall. The agony in my bones subsiding. I can relax, they'll be safe.

My eyes open, I see my parents. I'm three again. Skipping in my rough shirt and shorts. My bare feet slam on the grass. My mother rushes up behind me tickling my neck. I double over laughing, the soft gentle touch of her fingers on my skin. My father laughs running in to save me. I fly through the air as he swings me around in circles. Giggling, sparks flutter from my fingers from joy. The leaves flutter around us in the autumn breeze.

"My baby boy, come here." My mother takes me from my father and puts me upon her shoulders. I balance perfectly.

"Good boy." She holds my feet to steady me. My two unbroken goat horns sit on my forehead, my eyes glow.

I last no longer than a minute before I demand. "Down! Down!"

"What do you say, Enzo?"

"Please." I swing down to the ground and waddle forward.

"Enzo, can you get that apple." My father points to a tree, the apple hanging far above my three-foot body.

I concentrate on focusing my magic, it pops off the tree and whisks into my palm. I squeal in joy. "Mama! Dada! I did it!"

"He's getting good." My mother grins, pride in her eyes.

Gnawing my juicy apple, I beg. "Mama, you do it."

My mother rolls her eyes and all the apples in a mile radius drop to the ground. They thump like an echoing drum. The red blobs dart down like rain. I stare in awe. I'll do that one day. I will drop every apple in an orchard, like mama and I will chase rabbits with dada.

"Te amo." I hug my parents tightly.

My parents fade away from my grasp.

"No!"

I howl trying to clutch onto them for as long as I can but it's no use they fade to dust.

The forest disappears into the streets of Italy.

Margherita laughs at my joke, we walk down the cobbled street. The sun sets over the houses. Margherita yawns her frock strutting out ahead of her, her hair in a crown of curls. I walk slowly, enjoying the view of Italy. It has always been beautiful, the stone buildings tower overhead. Margherita links arms with me.

"You didn't have to walk me home," Margherita says in her thick Italian accent.

"I'll always be by your side," I reply, the streets are hardly safe enough to walk alone.

"Yes, you are."

"Is your husband-to-be ready for the wedding?"

"Actually, I have something to ask you." Margherita stops, holding both my hands.

"Of course."

Her eyes light up like diamonds in the moonlight. "Will you walk me down the aisle?"

My heart thunders in my chest. Margherita wants me to take her down the aisle. I can never imagine being able to have children of my own. I couldn't live with myself if they died. This is the closest I'll ever get.

"I'll be honoured."

Margherita squeals hugging me tightly. "Thank you! Thank you! Thank you!"

Happiness fills me. I embrace her back tightly.

My arms fall empty, I land in a ballroom. The room is made for a party, the Lord's mansion is gold and chandeliers decorate the ceiling. Laughter rings in my ears, I begin to spin. Music bursts in my eardrums. The song begins to play, the voice of an angel singing over the instruments and the drunken crowd. I twirl a beautiful woman and follow the dance steps I learnt so long ago. The woman giggles flirting shamelessly yet my eyes can't help following the young woman singing. A voice so beautiful it could bring you to tears. I spin the girl off to another man, eager for her attention unlike myself. She squeals as my magic sends her away. Quickly, I step away from the dance floor to near the platform where she sings.

The song ends and I pass her a drink. "What is your name?"

Closer, the woman is beautiful, bronze skin, soft brown eyes, hair curling to her shoulders.

"Ashley."

She sips the drink delicately, her eyes narrow. "Why are you here?"

"To tell you how beautiful your voice is, it's like an angel," I answer. "My name is Enzo Thornhill."

"I'm not for sale." Her voice grows cold at my compliment. "I'm already owned by a pig. He won't give me up so run along."

"What? I don't want to buy you."

I hate slavery. Selfish pigs need to pay for the work done for them. Humans are still humans no matter the colour of their skin. It is despicable. I cannot tell her this. She wouldn't believe me, I have to prove it.

"Who is your master?"

Her brow arches. "Lord Bastille."

I turn as worry goes over her face.

"Sir! I demand you step away from her. You. Sing now!" He glares in her direction.

Ashley jumps to sing, putting down the drink even though she has been singing for hours non-stop.

"Wait."

I raise my hands, sparks fly, Lord Bastille freezes in his place. Ashley's eyes widen in surprise.

"What should I do to you?"

I circle the Lord. None of the party guests seem to notice. They are entranced by the food, drink and people.

His head moves a few inches as he shakes. Ashley walks off the stage and over to him.

"He's frozen." In awe, she touches him.

"Yes."

"You aren't human." She states it bluntly, but doesn't seem to care. "Can I slap him?" She grins.

"You don't have to ask me to do anything."

After a moment of hesitation, Ashley takes a step back and her foot hits him right in the crotch. Tears pour down his cheeks. I laugh.

"Okay. You are going to let Ashley go. And all other slaves you may own. Or…"

Magic ignites in my palm. "Well, I think you get it."

I unfreeze him. The Lord is red-faced, wiping tears away. Ashley certainly packed a punch.

"Fine. Go. I'll set them free." He snarls. "Take the rest of the band with you!"

The band jump up from their seats and run off. They were all watching, but I don't believe they will mention to anyone that I am a warlock.

"Thank you!" Ashley wraps her arms around me.

I embrace her then put my arm out. "Do you wish to spend your first evening as a free woman with me?"

"Depends, will you really make sure he releases all his slaves?" She quizzes me.

"I can come back tomorrow and check." I have to give him a little time to release them but I'll stick with my threat.

Ashley links arms with me cheerfully. "Let's get out of here then."

Ashley's delighted face turns to dust before me.

I am sitting down with a crisp beer in my hand. The bartender polishes the wooden bar. The walls are a deep red, the lights flicker. I sit on a stool. Caterina beside me. I loved Caterina, she sought revenge with me till we were both satisfied. She is still alive, she is living in Africa. I keep meaning to visit her and meet her children, it is too late for that now.

"Look over there. She is totally checking you out." Caterina chugs her drink. I met Caterina when we were both trying to kill Trey Lester. Turns out we'd both been lab rats for the same stupid, curious humans. We have been firm friends since.

"I am not looking for anyone." I roll my eyes, three hundred years of life, love doesn't seem so desperate to find.

"Oh come on. She's pretty." Caterina winks at the girl in a cloak and cobalt blue dress.

"Are you looking for me or yourself?" I question her, while she stares at the girl.

"Challenge accepted." Her beer slams on the table.

"What challenge?"

"Both of us have to try to charm her, the winner is who she picks."

"I don't remember agreeing to this."

I look, I'm talking to myself. Caterina is already across the bar buying her a drink. I laugh. Oh, Caterina. She is picking a battle she cannot win, I'm much more charming.

My drink leaves my hand, the taste of crisp beer, the warm polished tavern all vanishes before my eyes.

"Enzo?" Colt's voice rings through the house.

"Yes?" I call.

Colt enters the kitchen while I am cooking. Cooking calms me, I cook when I have the time. I am an excellent chef. I just don't get to cook very often. Colt is pale, even for a vampire.

"I did something."

Colt drags me to the couch. A girl lies there, she has blood over her. My ears listen, she is breathing. I jump to her side, her eyes are closed. I don't have time to register who she is. I need to save her for Colt. The girl jumps from the couch. I howl, arms raising to use magic to kill the person. The girl laughs, high-fiving Colt. Abby turns to face me. A prank.

"You-" I swear to God. "I was going to kill you." I lower my hands.

Hell's Daughter

They laugh. "Sorry, Enzo. It was Colt's idea."

Abby grins. Colt's idea? I burst into a smile and shake my head. For Colt to be able to joke about being a vampire after Holly's cruel blow at him, that is a good thing. Abby is good for him, I'll admit. I chuckle and turn back to the kitchen. A fire blazes from the open oven. "Shit!" I curse. I absorb the fire with my fist. My eyes turn to red from orange.

"Oops." Abby laughs looking into the kitchen, it is burnt all up the walls.

Holly runs in, still holding a book. "Where is the fire? We have to get it out."

Snapping my fingers, the alarm goes off. I didn't even know it still worked.

Abby and Colt's laughter fades and there is Alex at my front door.

I stand there with the door half-open. "Hello?" I raise my eyebrow.

Alex is as beautiful as they say, also as reckless and smart I presume. But why is she at my door?

"You are the Hellhound Warlock, right?" Her eyes flutter to my appearance, not looking impressed.

"I prefer the name, Enzo Thornhill." I shrug.

"Do you know who I am?" She asks curiously.

"Yes." Everyone in the supernatural world knows who she is. Her family is the most powerful beings on Earth.

"Huh, everyone has bowed in my presence so far. Even demons." Alex lets a smile cross over her face.

"I can welcome you in, but I'm not bowing." I open the door far enough for her to come inside.

"Nice horns." She glides past. "Where did the other half of that go?"

"I'm not answering that." I use magic to shut the door behind us.

Alex strides herself across to my chair. "Not bowing, not answering questions. Don't you know royal etiquette?"

I roll my eyes. "I do but respect should be earned not given."

"I like that." She smiles.

"You are sitting in my seat."

"What are you going to do about it?" She teases.

I wave my hand, Alex flies across to one of the sofas. Alex laughs, two drinks appear. I quirk a smile. "Why did you come?"

"I need your help."

"With?" I prompt her.

"Banishing Lucifer. I overthrew him but keeping him in Hell is a lot of work. I need a binder to the Earth and Hell dimensions to seal his exit. You are the only known living creature tied to both."

"Huh, I wasn't expecting such a straightforward answer."

A shrug, she sips her scotch. "Will you help or not? I'll pay any price."

"I don't need material possessions."

Her eyes light up. "Is that a no?"

I chuckle. "I hate Lucifer, I'll do it for nothing."

"Really? Wow." Alex kicks up her feet. "I was ready to torture you till you broke. My morning has just opened up." She looks at her empty scotch, it refills. "Thanks. So, Enzo Thornhill is that your real name?"

"Yes, is Alex's yours?"

"No. Queen of Hell is my name."

I roll my eyes, I grin. Alex is not what I expected. She is not Lucifer, nor will she rule like him. I'm glad she has taken over. I trust she'll do good. I've never trusted anyone that quickly before. I hope I don't regret it.

My memories fade, stopping from playing under my eyelids. And the overruling blackness takes over one last time, cold tears fall relieving the pain.

CHAPTER FOURTEEN

Silven

My body starts to spasm, foam frothing at my mouth. No! I'm being un-possessed. How did they? Those bastards! I collapse. Out of the corner of my eye, I watch a pulse of magic explode from Enzo's chest then he falls. Dead. Cackling my body doubles over in pain. Shaking, a body doesn't matter to me now. The gate is almost open. I draw a nail soaked in my blood. I howl in pain. A pain worse than a million whips striking my back. I inch forward, hearing the stupid children cheer. I reach the edge of the circle and begin to draw the bird in the dirt. My eyes flutter. No! I need a little longer. A little, I try to finish the line. My shaking body stops. I feel my presence rip from the body. I scream. I begin to fall right back to Hell.

My eyes spring open, fire burning around me. The gate to Hell is opening. It is done.

Abby

I groan, I clutch my head, my entire body aching. What is going on? The last thing I remember is reading chained to Colt in Enzo's living room.

"Abby?"

"Yeah." I sit up from the ground.

"Oh my god. It's you!" Holly wraps her arms around me tightly.

"We stopped Silven." Holly rocks me.

"Really?" I hug Colt too.

Then I see over their shoulders. Bodies, more bodies and more. In rings of six around one singular body. I gasp, the smallest ring contains children. Innocent harmless children, brutally murdered. One has a circle of bruises around its tiny neck. One with stab wounds. More beaten to a pulp. My gut plunges. The children are no older than ten. They had their entire lives in front of them, they had barely started their lives. They never got the chance to grow up. They didn't deserve this fate. The adults are no different. Slit throats, broken bones. A tear slips down my cheek. I killed them all. I know it.

"Abby don't cry. It wasn't you. It was Silven. We stopped her. Lucifer isn't coming." Colt reassures me.

"You had no control," Holly adds.

My eyes fall to the body in the middle of the ring. Enzo.

"Did— Did I kill Enzo?" I squeal.

"What? No. He's unconscious. We'll catch you up later." Holly says. "He had to do the ritual to save us. We didn't let Silven finish."

I look at all the bodies. "We need to get to Enzo."

Carefully, without looking at the lifeless sad bodies we make our way to the centre. Colt moves aside a few children so we can sit with Enzo. He carefully shuts their eyes.

"I should warn you, Enzo won't remember anything. He said it would fry his brain."

Hell's Daughter

"What?" Colt and I exclaim.

"He told me it was worth it. We had to."

Colt nods grimly. "Enzo?" Enzo?"

No answer.

"Enzo?" I shove him. He doesn't respond. His eyes are glued shut.

"Why isn't he waking up?" I panic.

"Enzo!" Colt pushes him so hard he rolls on his side.

Blood pours from his nose, ears and eyes. Blood drips from his gawking mouth. Bruises cover his entire body. I have never seen Enzo so low.

"I can't hear a heartbeat!"

Colt panics grabbing Enzo by the chest, listening intently. A tear falls down his cheek. His heart has stopped. No that can't be right. He can't be dead. I grab his wrist feeling for a pulse. Nothing. My heart pounds, I killed him. I murdered Enzo.

"No! No! No!" Colt cries.

"No. He told me he'd lose his memories. Not...die." Holly's face falls.

Our victory is short-lived. Enzo can't die.

"We need Alex's blood. Enzo had some." I say. "He doesn't have to stay dead."

"We used it all." Holly shakes her head. "It was the only way to purge the demonic possession and Alex wasn't responding to Enzo."

"You are saying Enzo is truly dead? We can't get him back." Colt croaks.

Holly's mouth opens and closes the answer refusing to form. But from the look on her face, we already know the answer. Enzo is dead. He died for all of us, so we could live. To stop Silven. Tears well up in my eyes. Colt holds Enzo's hand crying. No sound coming from his lips. Shaking, he strokes Enzo's bloody knuckle. Though he makes no noise, I can feel his pain. Enzo shouldn't have died.

"No. No. No." Colt rocks back and forth.

Holly kneels by his body, in stunned silence. I can feel Colt's heartbreak. Enzo was his teacher, his brother, his friend, was always there for him and most of all believed him. I can only try to imagine how he feels.

"Enzo, I-I-" I can't speak, I want to apologise, but that won't bring him back. Damn it! I told him to kill me if necessary. He said he would do it, he lied. There must have been another way. He shouldn't have died.

Suddenly, the ground begins to shake beneath our feet. Enzo's body juddering. The earth crumbling under our fingertips.

Colt scoops up Enzo's limp body. "Run!"

We dart out the way, running down the path out the ritual site. The ground disappears under our feet. A slug-like, giant creature storms out from the gaping hole in the earth. Shit. Demon. Silven has opened the rift!

"Lucifer can escape." Colt curses. "We didn't do it."

My heart plummets. We failed. We failed Enzo.

Silven

Drooping down, I hit the dirt. Groaning, I roll gathering myself to my feet. I did it, the ground shifts opening the way to Hell.

"Silven." Demivda hisses. "You actually did it. Lucifer will be pleased."

"Yes, we need to get back to Earth, ready for Lucifer."

"Yes. Carolit is fetching him."

I nod. "Time to bring Hell and rule both dimensions."

The portal opens up, uncontrollable wind whisking over us. I smile, this is what it was like before Alex took control and the portal didn't have restrictions. We jump through with ease to wreak havoc again but worse this time.

Hell's Daughter

Demons jump through the rift, the stupid children are still here. You think they would run while they can. My eyes dance. Enzo lies dead in his son's arms. I have never been so happy to have killed someone. That death will always be my favourite. Shock masks all their innocent childish faces. They whisper, they thought they had stopped me. That's sweet. I chuckle. Colt's hands begin to shake. Slowly, he puts down Enzo's limp body. Enzo's face falls weakly. This is the first time Enzo has looked weak. I caused that, satisfaction courses through my veins. Demons hiss by my side. Alex hasn't made an appearance, probably running away knowing she can't defeat Lucifer again. Saving her own ass, the coward. Lucifer will take back his crown, he'll find Alex and kill her. I can't wait to see that. Revenge is always a wonderful sight. We should move these children out our way first. They've pissed me off enough. Colt's vampire teeth glimmer in the light. Looks like he isn't going to leave. Not that I mind. They have no hope. The air grows, swirling around me, time to end them.

Abby

Demons. A demon leads them, Silven I presume. They slither our way, a shiver goes down my spine. There is no way out of this.

"Lucifer is coming, isn't he?" I murmur.

Colt carefully lowers Enzo's dead body. He would have known what to do if he were here.

"Yes."

"What does he look like?"

"Human, like Alex only if you look him in the eyes, your soul will begin to die and wither," Colt answers, a growl in his throat.

"What do we do?" Holly asks in worry.

"Fight them in Enzo's honour."

"That is a suicide mission." Holly argues. "We had a hard time trying to kill one."

But there is no way out. They are faster than us and more deadly. We are dead meat. A demon begins to run our way.

"Shit!"

I feel for a weapon on my body, Silven didn't leave a single one. The demon charges. I duck behind a tree. Colt grabs it by the neck, ripping through the boiled dry skin with his teeth.

"Holly transform!" Colt urges, it's her only hope of survival.

"Abby, search Enzo for weapons!" His face clouds with rage.

They deserve to die. And Colt is willing to try and make it happen. So will I.

Holly's bones begin to crack. She whimpers in pain. Enzo had taught her to do that. Enzo pretended to be a jerk but he is the exact opposite and it resulted in his death. Kneeling with his body I put my hands in his pockets.

"Sorry," I whisper. I see a belt with a small pocket around his waist. I grab a knife from its holster and a note tumbles from his pocket. I unfold it. 'Colt, I'm sorry'.

I'm sorry, he is apologizing for dying. He knew he would die, he lied to Holly. I feel a fresh wave of tears. Damn it. My hand holds the blade tightly and I prepare to use it. A demon with eagle-like claws swoops at me. I duck, the talons scratch my back. They burn through the skin like fire. Enzo told me each demon can control one of the four elements. I guess this one has fire. The sharp chiselled beak goes straight for my chest. I block it with my knife. My heart beats manically the air is swarming with demons. The four turned to eight, then twelve.

My head spins as gusts of winds send me flying, fire scorches my skin, the cool icy relief of water washes over me. The ground shakes unsteadily under my feet. I try to breathe, the air pressure is constantly changing. My knife flashes in front of me. It all blurs together. There is no escape. I just have to keep fighting and have faith. Through the blur, I vaguely see Colt's mop of hair and a flying ball of fur which I pray is Holly. It's hard to see.

Hell's Daughter

Whenever I see a flair of fire, I wish it was Enzo but I know it's not. A tentacle comes flashing my way, I slash with my blade, cutting it in half while another wraps itself around my leg. The sharp sting as it clutches my leg makes me whimper. A demon snaps a furious beak my way, I stumble back over the tentacle. The weapon drops from my hand.

"No!" I call out as it gets kicked in the affray. "Crap!"

I'm dead. I'm going to die. Enzo saved us only for us to all fail and get ourselves killed. His death was for nothing. We've failed. I curse, the demons swarming around me. My knife is gone. Enzo's knife. I block a claw as it rips through my arm. I howl. I can't give up yet. I stomp on the tentacle holding me. The demon lurches back.

"Finish them!" Silven's slimy voice croaks.

I crawl out the way of a greasy faced monster, wax dripping from its body. Their skin is like flaky melted plastic. I scamper through feet, dodging blows. Damn it! I need a weapon. A blinding light stops me. I freeze, the beam of light slowly fades. I hear screams, they sound like a dying crow. The view clears. I see wings and horns in the sky. The horns are jet black, short and smooth. The wings are massive dark grey angel wings. Hair flowing over the woman's shoulder, wearing a leather jacket and jeans.

"Alex." I sigh in relief.

"Go back to Hell!" She screams at the frozen demons below her feet. The ground trembles at her touch. "Now!"

A shiver flies down my spine if I were them, I would be down in Hell in the blink of an eye. Alex has an aura around her, you can feel the power surrounding her.

"I said, go back to Hell or suffer the consequences!"

More than half the demons fade away into the rift. Colt stares frozen, Holly whimpers.

"You are all fools." Alex laughs at the fifty or so remaining. They charge.

Trinity-Rose Crane

Hell's Daughter

I duck out of the way, but I'm not fast enough. My jaw connects with a foot, I groan. A dagger finds my hand, Alex, I gather the little strength I have left, wield the dagger and stab a demon. The demon turns into a mothball at my feet. What the hell is this? Alex raises an arm, a demon chokes and withers away instantly. Why wasn't she here earlier? I lift the blade, the demon turns to dust. Two more swift gestures and the four of us are left with one demon, Silven.

"Lucifer is coming." She grins unaware she has lost.

"Why do you think it took me so long to show up? Lucifer isn't coming." Alex chuckles.

"N-no." Silven stutters. "He's coming. He's more powerful than you."

"Let me show you how powerful I am." Alex lifts and opens a hand.

Slowly, she closes a finger. Silven drops to her knees. The next finger sends Silven screaming.

"If Enzo were here, he would love to hear those screams." Alex's voice cracks at his name, hurt in her voice.

"Too bad I killed him." Silven laughs.

"Too bad you're going to die." The rest of the fingers close.

Silven screams, her body shaking and burning. Turning to ash and fading to nothingness. Alex didn't even touch her and now Silven is a few ashes blowing in the wind.

"Bastard demon." Alex kicks the pile of ash.

"How did you know Enzo was…" Colt chokes on the words weakly. "Dead?"

"It completes the ritual." Alex stares around the battlefield. "Where is his body?"

"There." Colt walks over to where Enzo's limp body lies.

Alex runs over and kneels by his body. "Enzo. I'm sorry." She cuts open her arm. "Why didn't any of you revive him earlier."

"He used all the blood to purge Silven from Abby."

Alex nods wordlessly, tears going down her cheeks, they fall on Enzo's face. My heart beats rapidly in my chest. Alex is saving

Enzo. He is going to live. I watch, I clutch both Colt and Holly's hands. The silence is deafening, waiting in suspense to hear his breath. A single gasp leaves Enzo's mouth.

CHAPTER FIFTEEN

Enzo

Gasping, I drink in oxygen. I knew Alex would come to save me.

"What took you so long?" I grin, propping myself up. "If it's revenge for the snails in your coffee, I swear that's petty even for you."

I feel weak but I'm alive. I had no doubts. Quickly, she rubs away the tears from her face.

"You died, and that is the first thing you have to say." Alex punches me playfully in the arm.

I laugh. "Didn't answer my question."

"I was securing Hell you asshole." She elbows me.

"Enzo?" A voice cracks. I look up, Colt wraps his arms around my neck. "Never die on me again."

I embrace Colt back. "I'll try not to."

Staring at the ash, blood and dirt, I see I have missed a grand battle. Colt eases back. "Promise not to sacrifice yourself again."

"I can't do that. What if I need to save your ass again?"

Colt smiles sadly. "You are an idiot."

I roll back my shoulder, I must have been dead for at least half an hour my joints are stiff. Abby smiles and steps forward.

"Thanks for-"

"Your welcome." I cut her off.

Slowly, I stand. Holly throws me a smile. I stare at the aftermath.

"I need to re-apply the ward."

Colt and Alex splutter behind me. "You have to be mad!"

"Is Lucifer stable? Unable to escape?" I ask.

Alex hesitates. "No, I won't let you do this again. You died."

"But you are here to resurrect me when I die." I smile "You think I'd have done that if I thought I would stay dead?" I joke.

Alex rolls her eyes. "Okay."

Colt nods. "Fine."

"I'll cover this up with the kids while you re-apply the spell."

Abby's face falls, she feels she killed them all. She can deny it but we all know it's a lie. We see a tragedy and she sees her own crimes.

"Can you save any of them?" I check.

"I can try, they might have been dead too long." Alex spins the dagger in her hand gracefully into her arm.

Colt and I stand ready, as I magic up the spell instructions.

"You died for me," Colt says as I read.

"And I'd do it again."

Colt smiles weakly. "I know. You are the only family I have. You always believe in me. I don't know what I would do without you having my back."

"You'll live your life, you are a good person. I have nothing else to teach you." I put down the paper. "You've been caring for Holly and Abby. You have done much better than I ever could have."

Colt falls silent as I begin the spell, magic surging through my veins.

Abby

Alex pours her blood into one of the children's mouth. My eyes widen and I watch his mouth open, gasping.

"Sit by the trees." Alex instructs.

The child brought back to life doesn't react. Instead, she nods like a robot and stands, and walking to the tree Alex pointed to sits down. The kid brushes her brunette hair out of her face silently.

"What was that?" I ask.

Alex stares deep in my eyes. "Sit down and put your hands up."

Against my will, I sit down and my hands go up. "You can do this to anyone?"

"Basically."

My arms drop and I can move my legs. "That's incredible."

"It's terrifying." Holly shudders. "You can make any human do whatever you want."

"Do I scare you?" Alex's eyes twinkle.

"Yes," Holly answers honestly.

"Good." Alex smiles. "And you?"

"I'd be scared if I was on the wrong side of you."

Alex laughs. "You'd be dead before you could be scared." Alex sighs. "There is an easier way to do this."

Her arms rise, all the bodies lift from the ground. She cuts her arm with a knife, the blood streams through the air to their mouths in channels. The funnel branches off, the cut in her arm seals up. Gasps one after another. My eyes watch as they wake up from death. Angel's power, all angels can do this, but they don't. People die all the time when they shouldn't. The angels don't help them all. They didn't help now. They pick who lives and who dies. That is scary.

"They won't remember anything. I promise." Alex answers the question I had been thinking.

Cutting open her arm, Alex offers it. "You look beat up. Take some."

I dab my fingers in the blood, I touch it on my tongue. I feel the relief flood through my body. The cuts and burns disappearing from my skin.

"Thanks. I'll check on the others."

Holly's eyes widen with a 'don't leave me with her' look.

"Come on Holly." Alex yells.

Walking over, Enzo finishes the spell. Colt smiles and walks over and strokes my arm. "Are you okay?"

I nod. "Yeah, you?"

"I'm good." Colt looks over to Alex who is talking to the people.

"I'll go for help." He jogs away.

Enzo murmurs in a language I don't understand. Sweat drips down his forehead, blood still stains his face, the broken horn surges with power as much as the other one does. Enzo's hands relax and it stops.

"It's done." Enzo wipes his face with his sleeve, it doesn't improve the sweat and blood covering it.

"Couldn't you whisk it away?" I wave my hand in a vague gesture to show how he uses magic. It was a bad impression of him by the way he laughs then shakes his head.

"Do you know how draining spells are? I've freed and trapped Lucifer in one day. I'm too weak to clean my face."

Enzo slumps against the tree and settles on the grass in exhaustion.

"Thank you." I sit next to him.

"For what?"

"You knew you'd die but you used all Alex's blood to save me."

Enzo shrugs. "I knew Alex would come."

"You saved all of us. And you would do it again. Even if you wouldn't be resurrected."

Enzo needs to stop being so humble.

"Yes. I would," he admits.

"Thank you. It means a lot." I tilt my head up to the sky. "I guess you didn't mean to when you said you would let me die."

"I meant it then." Enzo chuckles.

"I hope dying wasn't that bad."

Enzo's eyebrow shoots up. "It was the most painful experience I've ever had. Surely you know, you've died."

"My most painful experience was that blast when Silven ran."

"Sorry about that."

A pause. "What was it like? Dying?" I ask, I don't remember a thing. I was only gone for a few seconds.

"It was peaceful. I saw memories of those who I loved and cared about."

"Really?"

"Yes, I died happy and then I woke up."

I smile. That is good. Enzo stares at the grass, mind wandering somewhere else. He touches the tip of his broken horn.

"Did you see the moment you lost your horn?" I ask.

"No. That is what surprised me."

"How did it break?"

Enzo shook his head and moved away his hand. "I don't want to talk about it."

I see Enzo tense at the subject. He'll speak when he wants to.

The group waltz over, the group of sacrifices huddle in the corner.

"Enzo do you think you could portal these people home?" Colt asks.

Enzo groans. "I can try but I'm exhausted. You two should probably go home as well. It's sunrise."

Enzo waves at the two of us. "That is if I can make this damn portal." Struggling to his feet, Enzo sways gently.

Enzo

Alex offers her hand, I absorb her power. I take in enough power to create a universal portal that will send them all home even though I don't know where they live. The emerald green and sea blue portal shimmers before them all. Soaring through, one by one they return to their homes. Safe and sound.

Alex leans on my shoulder. I squeeze her hand, the power pumping through my veins. I wait for the mass of people to reduce till the last few zips by. Colt, Abby and Holly say goodbye and I send them home to rest. I close the portal. Alex keeps hold of my hand. I smile gently.

"I'm sorry I wasn't here," Alex whispers.

"I'm sure you had better things to do." I smile slyly.

She laughs. "Flint's kids needed protecting. They came after him. Turns out not all the demons like my ruling."

"You think?" I laugh, shaking my head. "It's because you have a heart," I answer.

"You could say that." Alex pulls back and looks me in the eye. "I'll answer your needy text messages next time."

"I'm not needy." I nudge her.

Alex smirks, but it's quick, she falls serious instantly. "Dying wasn't too bad was it?"

"No, I saw the most important people in my life. Some of them I haven't seen in a long time."

"Like who?" The twinkle in her eye returns.

"My parents, Ashley, Colt, Margherita, Caterina, somehow I also saw Abby and Holly."

Alex's shoulders droop, her grip on my hand loosening slightly. "Is that it?"

"No. There was one more person." I lean closer.

Alex grins her mischievous smile and lifts to her tiptoes. My lips touch hers and I kiss her gently. Alex grabs either side of my face, pulling me in and not letting go. Damn. The gentle soft kiss fades away and becomes more passionate and aggressive. I clutch her tightly, maybe there are benefits to dying. Gasping for air, the kiss breaks.

"I've been waiting forever for that," she whispers.

I chuckle. "I very much doubt that."

"For years then, stop ruining the moment," Alex growls softly.

"Very well." I kiss her again. Electricity sparks, my heart hammering in my chest. Alex kisses me hard. I wrap my arms around her waist, she has her hands on my shoulders feeling my shoulder blades. I sigh in sweet bliss. I didn't realise how much I wanted this until I'd died.

I pass over the bottle to Alex and she chugs the scotch. The wonderful view of Italy below us. We teleported to Rome. I swing my legs over the edge of the coliseum. Alex gives back the bottle.

"This is some good scotch. How long has it been aged?"

"Seven hundred years give or take." I swig it. "For it to be given a rating of 'good' by the top scotch connoisseur I think I picked the right bottle."

"You know what I like." Alex smiles, looking up at the moon. A few stars twinkle next to the half-moon. Slightly drowsy from the alcohol I yawn.

"Not a bad first date, huh?" Alex nudges me.

"Date? I thought I was just one of your hook-ups? I didn't think I'd see you after tomorrow."

"Damn you." Alex scowls.

"It's true you never call them back. You break their sad little hearts."

Alex shoves me harder, I sway leaning out to see the long way down to the stone paving. The old rocks crumble slightly at my touch. The rock where my hand sits crumbles. A chunk breaks off. I slip, tumbling over the ledge. Air whooshing past me, the wind stinging my face. I laugh, the ground growing closer, till I am only a storey high. I still don't stop. A few inches away from the concrete. I pause in mid-air.

"You could save yourself, you know?" Alex hovers beside me.

"That is no fun." We float back up to the top and settle back on the rocks.

Alex smiles, her eyes fall on my horns. "I've always admired you for wearing your horns. I would do it but wings and eyes that reflect Hell might scare humans a little too much."

"You should do it." I encourage her. I would love to see that.

"I can imagine the newspaper already." Alex laughs, then reaches out to touch my broken horn. "I've always wanted to know what happened."

I grimace. "Do you want to know?"

"If you'll tell me."

I close my eyes. My hand touches Alex's and we vault into my head. Soaring through the memories.

I struggle in the chains that wrap around my wrists. I'm ten years old. My clothes are rags, too small for me now. I shiver, my hands spark with magic. Tiny sparks that fizzle out and fall. I'm too weak to do more than that. My stomach growls, my ribs stick out under my shirt and my spine hurts from the hard metal bed.

"No." My croaky voice begs.

My parched mouth wouldn't allow anymore sound. I get a cup of water a day with a little bit of food. Enough to live but not enough to be capable of magic. I stopped eating at one point, I'd much rather die than stay here but then they force-fed me. I am a lab rat for some crazy scientist who killed my parents. They killed my parents and took me alive for experimentation. My side burns from where they have taken my flesh with a knife. To see if my DNA is different from a human's.

They want to get rid of supernaturals for good. They want a cure. They want to turn all the monsters to humans. A monster, that is what they call me. In my opinion, they are the monsters. They are killers. My parents did everything they could to protect me, but the scientists had help. My parents died in my arms. There was a bloodbath. I fought back with all my strength. I failed them. It's been years I can only track the day by their systematic tests. They record each day on their machines.

We are on 'day 1296' I'm not sure how many years that is. They pull out a syringe. The green liquid in the vial looks deadly. My eyes widen. What is that? They normally take blood samples, perform tests to find triggers. They measure my heartbeat, a few more torture techniques. Force me to change. They've pumped unknown drugs into me to see a reaction. This looks like a drug they have made. I squirm.

"No."

"Enzo. Enzo, stop moving." The doctor clamps my arm.

"No. Please." I whimper helplessly.

I have no choice, I'm tied to a metal table with restraints.

The cold needle goes through my skin, injecting into my veins. The green liquid enters my system. Spasming, I lose control of my body. Shaking violently, my eyes roll back in my head. Pain, pure agony rips through my body. I have never felt anything like it. A burning sensation through every cell. Not like a natural fire from Hell. This is like poison through my entire body. As if acid was flowing through my veins. Tears roll down my cheeks, my skin catches fire, a pale green colour. I can't speak, I scream out for help. My stomach churns, daring to make me throw up. My skin boils, burns appear. I can feel them under my skin. This shouldn't happen. This is not natural. With all my effort, I clench my fist. I feel blood in my palms where my uncut nails dig in. I try to absorb the fire, I should be able to. I am part Hellhound. I close my eyes tight, biting my tongue to stop the screams. I whimper against my will, my eyes burn with tears. My eyes open to a blinding light, my head pangs, my ears buzz. Magic out of my control surges in pulses from my body. Glasses smash, the doctors smack into the wall. Clipboards fly. My goat horns hold static energy. I hear a crack, I emit magic like a beacon. Choking, I can't breathe. My body burns from the inside out. I feel fire and magic course through my veins. A crack in my horn, my tiny body unable to contain the energy I wield.

Jolting away, I lift my arm. It's free from the tight hold of chains. The molten mess oozes over my hand. Small pieces of black dust cover my chest. I sit up, staring in the mirror. My horn is broken. Half of one shattered to pieces. I touch it gently. Magic flies from my fingers uncontrollably. This isn't natural magic. A bell rings. The doctor lies dead on the floor. More are coming. I smile, time to avenge my parents.

We come out of my memory. Alex keeps hold of my hand. "You didn't let me see the good part."

"Which is?"

"You avenging your parents and your childhood like a badass."

I laugh. "You can see that if you want."

Alex bounces excitedly. I close my eyes and replay the scene.

I remember it vividly. Bloodshed, I burnt the doctors to a crisp. I couldn't control the amount of magic pulsing out my body. I didn't have to lift a finger and they fell to the floor. The serum made my powers unbelievably strong. Blood, guts, brains, and lost limbs spread throughout the building. None of them lived. My entire body buzzing with power, I reached the locked doors to freedom. The power charged from my body, sending a wave that collapsed the building to a wreck.

Alex grins. "You are a badass!"

I chuckle.

"You burnt right through that woman's head while she begged you," Alex says in astonishment. "I knew you were notorious for seeking revenge. You spent three hundred years of your life in dedication to it."

"I did, you like your revenge as well." I point out.

"I do." She grins tilting her head into my shoulder. "They are the best of days."

We fall silent, for a moment. Enjoying the cold night air, the crescent moon.

Alex swigs the scotch. "When I came to your house the first day we met, I thought you would try and kill me."

"Tempting," I smirk.

"Hey!" Alex shoves me gently.

"I'm kidding. No. I'd heard you were ruling Hell and I was very happy about it."

"Why?"

"Fishing for compliments I see. You aren't a ruthless maniac like your father. Like the plague was a bad idea. What was he thinking? Your brother, Flint, he couldn't do shit to control demons. He's kind. You are the steady median."

Alex chuckles. "Good point."

"I know." I down the last of the bottle. The bottle disappears into thin air. I can feel my magic coming back to its full strength. Slowly but surely. A hand touches my face and then lips aggressively press on mine.

Abby

I walk into the half-burnt down house. The wall to the garage is blown open, glass is broken. Colt's van sits outside the empty garage. There is a car missing. "Where is the car?"

"Silven destroyed it when she took Enzo off-road."

"What? You need to tell me everything Silven did."

"Yeah. That's a long story." Colt goes into the house.

Following him inside, I look up where the chandelier used to be, there are now iron chains hanging from the ceiling, the glass in splinters on the floor. Furniture is broken, strewn across the room. Enzo's favourite chair is smashed to pieces. The armrests are on opposite ends of the living room. There is a table blocking the way to the kitchen.

"Did I do this?" I look around at the mess. Glass crunching underfoot.

"No. Enzo did it in a massive rage." Holly carefully walks through it.

I look up, there is a gaping hole in the ceiling. Bricks lie on the floor in chunks. "Does Enzo normally do this when he's angry?"

"No. Normally he can control it." Colt touches a scorched wall.

"But I was very pissed off." Enzo comes through a portal.

Alex gazes around with a smile. "Damn, you torched this place. I'm impressed."

Alex walks in. "Wow. Why is your garage empty?"

"The car is a wreck," Enzo replies.

"I told you, you need back-ups."

Enzo rolls his eyes at her.

"You got very mad." I wave to the room. Well, what is left of it.

"And you were trying to teach me anger management?" Holly laughs. "I had to calm you down."

"Yeah." Enzo wracks his hands in his hair.

"I'm surprised you were able to stay this calm." Alex gazes at the room. "Keeping your powers in control must be difficult. I mean, you got injected with a serum that made you crazy powerful."

"I've had hundreds of years to gain control of it. I should have been able to contain it."

I look to Enzo in surprise. I didn't know that, there is a lot I don't know about him. But I'll get to know him. Colt takes my hand. I squeeze it hard. The glass disappears, the walls begin to repair themselves around us, Alex snaps her fingers and decoration appear.

"Wait? You can do magic?" I ask in surprise.

"Sort of. It's complicated."

I laugh, I get that. This entire supernatural world is complicated. Yawning, I collapse on the sofa with Colt.

"Too tired to celebrate?" Alex shakes a champagne bottle.

A faint snore, Holly is curled up in the corner fast asleep.

"I think that is a yes." Colt chuckles. "We should all sleep."

"Agreed." Enzo looks at Holly. "I'll magic her to a guest room. "There are more down the hallway." Enzo offers.

"Thanks."

Lying in bed, I wrap my arms tightly around myself. I'm me again. Silven has no power over me and it feels good. Knowing she had control to take over me at any second is terrifying. Yet they all stuck with me. Even Enzo who promised to kill me if it got too bad didn't. He saved me, till it killed him. Colt and Holly took down Silven by themselves to save me and bring me back. I take a deep breath, I can't sleep. I sit up and hug my knees. It's been over a day since I've slept. I should be sleeping like a log. I perch at the end of the bed. I wear new pyjamas Enzo made for me. A knock on my door sends me jumping in the air. I land hard on the floor, groaning.

"Come in!" I call, scampering off the floor.

Colt laughs. "Did I scare you?"

"Possibly. Can't you sleep either?"

"No." Colt walks in.

I pat the bed next to me, he climbs in. We sit, me leaning on his shoulder. Colt instantly yawns, and in a minute of silence, I hear a quiet snore.

"Colt?" I whisper.

No answer. I chuckle so much for not sleeping together. A shiver rolls down my spine. I rub my arms against the cold. I pull the duvet up and close my eyes. Colt's ice-cold hand intertwines in mine. I can finally sleep. I'm safe.

Lucifer

I laugh, the cackle echoing in the realm of Hell. Alex, my wimp of a daughter still hasn't got the power to kill her dear old dad. Even at my near return, she couldn't do it. My finger's snake around the bars. They burn my hand gently. I'll escape soon, this cell won't be able to hold me much longer. I have followers.

Silven the most loyal is dead, she was also foolish. I knew her plan would fail. No matter how many times she whispered it to me through the bars. Her actions weren't pointless luckily, she did have a use. I have a new holding cell, the small stir she created will help me greatly. I listen intently to every whisper, every step of a demon. Methodically I plan my escape. Silven thought I needed to escape Hell. She thought I needed Earth to succeed. I don't. I'm right where I need to be. She had the right idea about the boy, but I shall use him another way.

Two cheerful voices ring my way. Here they are now. Alex and the one person other than her brother she has ever trusted. My half angelic daughter turns the corner. That's her problem. Angel blood, she is too pure to live in Hell let alone to rule it. She has a heart, I scrunch my nose at the words. My son is no better and he's a full demon. I thought he would be my shot at a powerful loyal evil child. One I could be proud of, but he has more of a heart than she has. A heart is for the weak. It makes individuals vulnerable.

"What do you want me to do?" The boy, Enzo, asks.

Alex doesn't even glance in my direction. The hatred and anger boil in my veins. Only for me to grin. Anger only makes the kill sweeter. I am one step closer. The girl Silven possessed, she may be purged of demonic energy but she is a key. A shimmer of light in the rift that opens Hell to Earth. She finishes the spell to open it. She can reopen it. Like a key in the lock but they are too stupid to know.

That is why I encouraged Silven's plan and sent the werewolf after the twin. The two girls have dormant witch blood in their veins, the human girl now has demonic energy too. Enzo, the bastard child, he lifts his warlock hands. His magic is unique. It'll become an advantage or disadvantage, depending on how I play my cards.

"Just make sure he can't break out." Alex snarls.

My dead soulless eyes stare deep into hers. Lover boy snaps sparks in my direction. The forcefield around my cell goes purple and blue as he works. A moment later, he stops. His hands flicker, I soar, slamming into the bars. My face burns. I refuse to howl in pain. Dropping my body, the boy scowls. He has spirit, I like that. Adds to the challenge. Twisting my head, I look into his eyes. Most people would squirm away, Enzo stares right back into mine. I can smell the horrors of his life, every ache or yearning. Enzo acts like a good man, loyal Hellhound Warlock but I can see further within. There is more to him. Not just the revenge and anger he fought for his entire life something even better. Evil. Of the worst kind.

I laugh, the boy is only five hundred years old but wise. It'll be sweet revenge once he is on my side. He is the only man my daughter has ever loved. I can smell it on her. The pair leave without another word. They will be seeing me a lot sooner than they think...

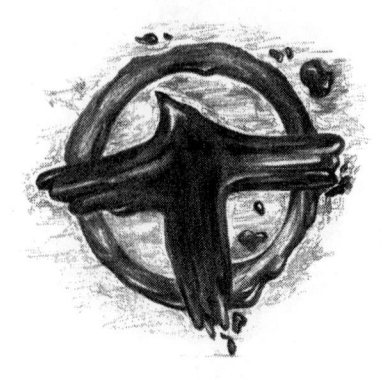

Trinity-Rose Crane

ABOUT THE AUTHOR

Trinity-Rose is a teenage writer from Hampshire in the UK who lives off coffee and bubble tea to function as she spends most of her nights thinking up her next book idea. She is the third child and currently lives with her parents, younger sibling and border collie called Izzy. From the age of ten she started writing her own short stories for her family.

The passion of writing came from her love of reading books. She found her love of the supernatural after reading Kelley Armstrong's young adult books in her early teens. This made her want to create her own supernatural world with exciting relatable characters who are fond of sarcasm. She also enjoys incorporating her love of sports cars into her books. The love for sports cars is thanks to her dad who for her fifteenth birthday, took her for an experience day to drive sports cars around a race track.

Trinity-Rose spent most of her early teen years either at school, writing or hanging out with her best-friend who she met on the first day of nursery. At school she was either talking to friends, learning or jotting up notes for her books. Ironically she got better grades in Maths than English.

When it came time at school to consider career paths she looked at becoming a scientist or lawyer but quickly changed her mind when she realised she wouldn't love it as much as writing and decided to devote all her time to dreaming up stories she could share her work with more than just her family and friends. This inspired her to write her first novel *Hell's Daughter*.

OTHER BOOKS BY THIS AUTHOR

For The Latest Information On

New Releases

&

Coming Soon

Please Visit

JasamiPublishingLtd.com